GREAT HOTELS
OF PARIS

GREAT HOTELS OF PARIS

BERNARD
ETIENNE
and
MARC
GAILLARD

This book would not have been possible without
the generous help of Monsieur Pascal Boissel.

The Vendome Press • **New York**

Translation : Catherine Henry and Veronica O'Brien.
Copyright © ÉDITIONS ATLAS, Paris, MCMXCII.
All rights reserved.

First published in French in 1992 by ÉDITIONS ATLAS s.a.,
89, rue La Boétie, 75008 Paris, France.

First published in the United States of America by
The Vendome Press, 515 Madison Avenue, New York, N.Y. 10022.
Distributed in the United States of America and Canada by
Rizzoli International Publications, 300 Park Avenue South, New York, N.Y. 10010.

Library of Congress Cataloging-in-Publication Data Étienne, Bernard.
    [Palaces et grands hôtels de Paris. English]
    Great hotel of Paris / by Bernard Étienne and Marc Gaillard. p. cm.
    Translation of : Palaces et grands hôtels de Paris.
    ISBN 0-86565-139-6
    1. Hotels, taverns, etc. --France--Paris. I. Gaillard, Marc. II. Title.
TX910.F8E8513 1993
647. 94443'6--dc20
                                                          92-28065
                                                             CIP

I have always seen luxury hotels as legendary places. When you come from a working-class suburb in Marseilles, the great hotels on the Côte d'Azur belong to another world. Until, that is, you enter that other world, and find that dream has become reality.

So there came a time when I began to use luxury hotels, even felt more or less at home in them. Yet, what do I mean by "at home"? Home is somewhere that belongs to you, and God knows I was thrilled when I was able to buy my first house. Then, gradually, ownership became a burden.

I owned Roquefort, the place I bought between Vence and Grasse. Eventually I lost interest in it, stopped going there, didn't want to know about it. When I sold it, it was a relief, though I was a bit sad too, because that's the kind of person I am.

Being in a great hotel is the very opposite of owning a house : it's anonymous luxury, with everything perfectly organized. I feel free, I feel alive. I'm caught up in the rhythm of the place, the whirl of departures and arrivals, I'm just one among so many others, and still I feel myself recognized as an individual. The people at the hotel know me, they're on my side, somehow or other they convey this to me. That's what being "at home" really means to me ; it's the little extra sense of being "me" that I have in a hotel.

And so, when they tell me that these dream places have a soul and a history, when they say the Prince of Wales came to this bar or Hemingway to that, when they show me Charlie Chaplin's sittingroom, Marlene Dietrich's suite, or Greta Garbo's, I believe all I'm told. I plunge straight into that world of memories. All that kind of thing is magic for me, it makes me feel better, and that's what's important. When I arrive at the Martinez, the Negresco or the Lutétia, I smile at the porter, not to show off, but because I look on him as my guardian angel.

And that's all part of the history of luxury hotels too. Their legend isn't created by famous names in the visitors' book, but by the way they treat you. In the last analysis, it's not only money or organized luxury that count, it all comes down to style and talent. What luxury hotels have to offer is work well done plus knowing how to make life worth living.

César

THE BRISTOL

Ultimate luxury

Fashions come and fashions go, even in the fairy-tale world of great hotels ; their livelihood depends on the unpredictable butterfly whims of their clients. Their flights of fancy may tip the balance of success, for the customer, of course, is always right.

There are "however" one or two places untouched by the swings of fortune ; places whose clients return again and again, having no truck with the modish recommendations of tourist guides. The *Bristol* is one such place.

One generation of clients follows another to the *Bristol* with amazing fidelity. These are the kind of people a hotelier dreams of ; people who exclaim with pleasure in the restaurant as the waiter lifts the silver covers. But that pleasure is not produced by accident. It is just one mark of the intimate luxury offered in a hotel that succeeds in appearing timeless while keeping abreast of the latest developments.

The *Bristol* is famous for its golden silence. No sound is heard other than a little quiet piano music at cocktail time, a little gentle conversation and tinkle of china cups at tea time. In the public rooms – how incongruous that expression seems – there is never any sense of being overwhelmed by the sort of intimidating grandeur one sometimes finds elsewhere.

Let us imagine that we have arrived at 122 rue du Faubourg-Saint-Honoré. After giving the keys to the man who will put our car away, we pass through the great revolving doors into the care of the valet who will see to our luggage and our room-keys. The foyer makes an excellent first impression. As we admire the pillars, the couches, the paintings, the Bohemian glass of the chandeliers, we

may think of the celebrities who have admired them before us, people like Marilyn Monroe, Ava Gardner, and countless others who have had the same welcome from M. Lainé, head porter for more than forty years.

This four-star luxury hotel, with its garden *à la française* and its hushed atmosphere reminiscent of a more gracious age, is more like a great private house, where guests feel as if this were their own home, as if they were being waited upon by their own servants.

This book could not provide enough space to accommodate the stories of the founders and owners of all the hotels it presents. Yet there must be some exceptions, as in this case ; when the mark of the founder is ineradicably present. Could Hippolyte Jammet return to the *Bristol* today, he would certainly be delighted to find that after half a century his rule of conduct is still followed to the letter : "For a good hotelier, the details are what count".

Each one of the two hundred and ninety-five members of staff provides a standard of service which is old-fashioned in the best sense of the word. Clients are treated with great respect, surrounded at all times by the most meticulous attention to their requirements. Such attention is an art in itself, because of the ever-present danger of its sliding into obsequiousness. From the moment of setting foot in the foyer, the guest is taken in charge, in a manner which is one of the secrets of the house. For instance, a regular visitor may be sure that his likes and dislikes are kept on record. The chambermaid will have reported the time he wishes to be called in the morning, what he takes for breakfast, what news-

paper he reads. The Jammet family, now retired from business, has left its mark, for its intention had been to found an upper-class family hotel. The new management has fully maintained that intention in carrying on the proud tradition of the *Bristol*.

Since we are in the foyer, which looks exactly as it did on the day the hotel opened, let us admire the beauty of the twenty-three Baccarat crystal chandeliers, the Carrara marble floor with its great 19th century Savonnerie carpet, the Louis Seize armchairs and couches upholstered in rich Lyon silk. Various pieces of furniture, precious objects and trinkets were acquired at auction between 1924 and 1930. These treasures,many of them thrown up by the upheavals of the Great War, were personally chosen by Hippolyte Jammet, whose ex-

Above : the singer Jessie Norman is a regular visitor at the Bristol. Opposite : the winter restaurant, also called the dining-room, in the 1960s, with its oval glass roof still in place. Below : the same dining-room today, restored and redecorated. One of the best restaurants in Paris.

cellent taste thus provided the *Bristol* with much of its present wealth of collector's pieces. The collection was enlarged in 1950 – after yet another war – by an even greater number of acquisitions.

Napoleon's mother, Letitia Ramolino, received from her son the gift of a Gobelins tapestry representing Meleager, king of Calydon in Greek mythology. It now hangs in the *Bristol*. Opposite a bust by Pajou of her husband Louis XVI, a painting of Marie-Antoinette by Drouhais has pride of place. The portrait was given by the Queen herself to her confessor, Mgr Duchilliau, bishop of Chalon-sur-Saône. Two splendid pictures by J.-B. Pater adorn the entrance to the restaurant. It is not possible to list all the art treasures such as Flemish tapestries and period furniture in the bedrooms and suites. It is an indication of the quality of the clientele that no harm has ever come to any of these items.

What was once a charming oval eighteenth century theatre seating four hundred people is now the winter restaurant, almost exactly as it was when it first opened. Glass richly worked with gold-leaf tracery filters a gentle daylight which may once have fallen on Kim Novak or Rita Hayworth in their great days. In this restaurant, acknowledged as one of the most beautiful in Paris, where perfectly appointed round tables are set well apart, memories of the stars of yesterday do indeed come to mind as the stars of today arrive to dine in epicurean anonymity. The panelling of Hungarian oak following the curve of the walls was worked and polished in 1942 by a team of twelve sculptors under the direction of the Jewish architect Lherman, whom M. Jammet took under his wing during the war.

The "Four Seasons", painted in the same period by Gustave-Louis Jaulmes, the Swiss who de-

corated the salle Pleyel, has its themes and colours repeated on the console tables in magnificent flower-arrangements renewed every morning. Jaulmes belonged to the school of Maurice Denis, who, like Gauguin, was a great Symbolist painter, and Denis's influence is evident here in the many delightful intimist pictures. Thr *Bristol* has some amusing features peculiar to itself. You may, for instance, happen by chance on a garden *à la française* set in a huge courtyard of twelve hundred square metres, and leading to the summer restaurant. Nowhere in Paris is there anything comparable to it, nor to the incredible covered swimming-pool on the roof of the hotel, looking out over the Sacré-Cœur, the Elysée palace and the diplomatic quarter. Among the hotel's minor amenities, it is worth noticing the wrought-iron lift of which it is justifiably proud.

How this building came into existence is a complicated tale. François Jammet was a Catalan who worked in Paris during *la Belle Epoque*, first as a chef in the *Hôtel des Deux Mondes*, then as owner of the well-known *Boeuf à la mode*, before going to Dublin to found a restaurant that was considered the best in that city for many years. So his son Hippolyte was reared in the Irish tradition. Hippolyte returned to France in 1914 to join the army, and after the war he bought the *Bellevue*, a small hotel in avenue de l'Opéra.

In the galloping inflation of the post-war years, he sold it some time later for five times what he had paid, and then bought at 112 rue du Faubourg-Saint-Honoré the Hôtel de Castellane, a town house which had once belonged to Madame de Pompadour, mistress of Louis XV. After restoration work

which took two years, it opened its doors to the public in 1925 as the *Bristol*. The hotel was built in the purest Eiffel style, as was then the fashion, with iron girders, and ill-wishers called it the first scrap-iron hotel in Paris ! Jammet was also criticized for having destroyed a historic building. No doubt he did. Still, he was about to make history in his turn, as owner and manager of the new building, as a hotelier in the best sense of the term.

At the end of the nineteenth century, hotels called *Bristol* could be found by the score all over Europe. The popularity of the name was due to Frederick Hervey, count of *Bristol*, bishop of Derby, friend of Goethe and of Voltaire. This great Irish traveller spent half of his time on horseback, the other half in the best hotels on the continent, where he was known as "the vagabond star".

One of the suites with its sitting-room, period furniture and toile de Jouy curtains.

He was such a lavish spender that several hostelries took their name from his title, doubtless as a mark of gratitude, so forming what may be described as the first chain of hotels long before such an idea had been heard of. However, by 1925 the name was dropping out of fashion, and when a hotel so called in the Place Vendôme closed down, Hippolyte Jammet was only too pleased to reclaim the name and restore it to its ancient glory, in honour of his own cherished connections with Ireland.

He was taking a risk, for the Faubourg-Saint-Honoré was almost in the suburbs, far from the Champs-Elysées towards which rich visitors were inclined to gravitate. To be sure, the official residence of the President of the Republic was nearby ; still, this part of the city was traditionally connected with banking rather than with entertainment. Jammet used this apparent handicap to his advantage by providing diplomats and aristocrats alike with the kind of comfort and discretion they required. Was it by a miracle that, unlike other hotels in the same category, the *Bristol* was neither

The Bristol was first in the field with telex equipment. Hippolyte Jammet and his son Pierre (above) were quick to recognize the value of the new technology. Left : The magnificent French garden with its pillars and fountains.

on the menu at the *Bristol* in a time of food rationing. There were no vacancies in the place which became known as the "Diplomats' Hotel", where twelve ambassadors and their staff were working while waiting to return to their embassies. No hitch in the electricity supply either, since the hotel was on the same grid as the Elysée ; it could even operate the air-conditioning system which had been installed in 1930, well in advance of rival establishments. The *Bristol* was also first in the field with a telex service. It could even provide an anti-gas shelter, should the need arise.

While the *Bristol* was regarded as a reliable base in those difficult times, it had not yet achieved the prestige it began to enjoy some years later, when a new generation of the Jammet family took charge. Special credit must go to Pierre, the eldest of ten children, who was to guide the fortunes of the hotel from 1964 to 1978, and bring it to a new eminence. Perhaps all this was pre-ordained for a man born the year the hotel opened, and whose first cradle was a drawer from an Art Deco chest in room 101 !

A hotel which aims to reach the top and to stay there is obliged to maintain the most rigorous standards. Every year up to 1965, seven or eight bedrooms were entirely renovated, and new bathrooms were installed, each with its bath and shower. Always full of new ideas, M. Jammet introduced a new form of refinement by equipping the bathrooms with magnifying mirrors with built-in lighting. Another important event was the promotion from basement to foyer of the staff responsible for entering reservations in a day-book. Which produced this pithy comment in the hotel's records : "Today the day-book has seen the light !". Another step forward was the acquisition of the convent next door, when the Sisters of the order of Bonne-Espérance left to establish a house in Canada. That allowed a new wing to be built. Yet another wing, now called *La Résidence*, was added in 1978, when the convent cloister was transformed into the garden *à la française* mentioned earlier. Ten years later, a still more extensive renovation programme in the old part of the hotel updated about sixty bedrooms, ten of them suites. The overall intention was always to do better, and then to do better still.

Today, there are two hundred bedrooms and forty-four suites in the *Bristol*, all furnished with re-

damaged nor requisitioned during the Second World War ? Not only that : it never closed. What happened was that, while rival hotels were being taken over by the occupying forces, Hippolyte Jammet had a brilliant inspiration. He approached the American embassy, still neutral at the time, and offered it the use of his premises. It goes without saying that the offer was accepted : who could turn down such a princely gift ? And so it came about that in 1942, when all the other major hotels were in German hands, the *Bristol* enjoyed the privileged position of playing host to Allied ambassadors and their advisers, indeed in effect to the whole diplomatic corps. Which does not mean that diplomats were the only guests during the war. Various wellknown personalities found refuge there too, like, for instance, Cécile Sorel, a French actress who had played with distinction at the Comédie-Française in "Le Misantrope" and "Le Mariage de Figaro", and later on the music-hall stage.

After the Liberation, its proximity to the Elysée and the Ministry of the Interior helped to put meat

The great Cécile Sorel made the Bristol her home while she was working at the Comédie Française and later at the Casino de Paris.

markable taste and variety. Particularly fine are the Art Deco goblets by Lalique, wonderful examples of glass-making skill in the 1920s. All the bathrooms – the hotel always lavishes the most loving attention on its bathrooms – are in white marble and equipped with heated towel-rails; toilet accessories and bath oils are by Hermès. There is even a system of background music to soothe the nerves !

The bedrooms in *La Résidence* are specially designed to be both functional and luxurious. Some have balconies; almost all look out on the restful garden. They are clearly intended to suit the taste of the rich businessmen, the international bankers and other financial experts who now make up the bulk of the hotel's clientele. Intelligent planning of the position of doors and provision of independent entrances has made it possible to accommodate these guests in private self-contained units. In the main building, no bedroom is like any other. Many of them look like museums of furniture. Yet none of the precious items – tapestries, chests of drawers, carpets – has ever suffered as much as a scratch, much less has there ever been any question of theft. This happy state of affairs is of course a tribute to the quality of the guests, a quality which the management takes every care to maintain and protect. So it was that, some years ago, two well-known foreign actors were invited to feel the need for a change of air after a display of aggressive behaviour and verbal abuse. That is surely the ultimate luxury for a hotel – to be able to choose its clients rather than the reverse.

In the 1950s, when the well-to-do classes on the international scene discovered the *hauts couturiers* and luxury shops opening along the Faubourg-Saint-Honoré, they moved into the *Bristol* for their receptions and cocktail parties. Winter brought the South-Americans, followed in Spring by the Egyptian cotton tycoons, who came no more after the fall of king Farouk, himself a frequent visitor to the *Bristol* as well as to the *Royal-Monceau*. When the future king Faisal of Iraq (assassinated in 1958) and his cousin king Hussein of Jordan were at school in Eton, they always stayed at the *Bristol* when they came to Paris, accompanied by family and retainers.

The arrival of a transatlantic steamer at Le Havre was an important event for the hotel. The *Bristol* was a "must" for many millionaire tourists and businessmen arriving from the United States

14

of America and setting foot for the first time on French soil. Not a bad place to start from ! But you needed to have booked a year in advance.

The *Bristol* had reached its zenith by 1960. It received a great diversity of clients, such as the Greek shipping magnates Goulandris and Niarchos, the celebrated conductors Herbert von Karajan and Igor Markevitch, Mrs Mallowan (better known as Agatha Christie), and Professor Barnard. The cinema world was likewise affected by "*Bristol* mania" : Judy Garland, Julie Andrews, Jennifer Jones, Merle Oberon, Ursula Andress, Maria Montez, Maureen O'Hara, the shapely "barefooted contessa" Ava Gardner; these all came, as did John Wayne, Orson Welles, Alec Guinness, James Stewart, Kirk Douglas, Jean-Pierre Aumont, Paul Anka, William Holden and Charlie Chaplin. Chaplin stayed there only once, preferring, it seems, the arcades in rue de Rivoli.

One evening is remembered with particular poignancy. On the 8th of April 1975, the great Josephine Baker gave a party at the *Bristol*, with Princess Grace of Monaco as one of the guests, to celebrate her return to the stage at Bobino. A few days later, Josephine Baker was dead.

Politicians were noticeably faithful to the *Bristol*, no doubt because of its convenient location. Many meetings were held there, official and unofficial; many suppliants for political favours sat there for long hours. After the end of his period of office as President of the United States, Harry Truman came with his wife and daughter to stay at his friend Hippolyte Jammet's hotel. Whatever the outcome of their official negotiations, foreign statesmen knew they could depend on the *Bristol* to look after their personal comfort : Harold Macmillan,

Josephine Baker (seen here with her friend Princess Grace of Monaco) gave a reception at the Bristol to celebrate her latest come-back. A few hours later, Josephine was dead. A portrait of Marie Antoinette by Drouhais may be seen in this salon where the reception was held.

Harold Wilson, Anthony Eden, Edward Heath, Lord Mountbatten from Great Britain, Ben Gurion and Golda Meir from Israel, Robert MacNamara and Henry Kissinger from the United States. Kissinger is still a regular visitor today. The names of Sadat and Tito also figure in the visitors' book. There is no doubt that a part of post-war history was made here. But the *Bristol*, of course, is not saying ; as always, discretion is its watchword.

It is perhaps not too great an intrusion into Pierre Jammet's private life to mention that he was twice married, and on each occasion to a German wife. This connection helped to spread the fame of his hotel across the Rhine. Ever since 1950 the *Bristol* has been receiving distinguished guests from the Federal Republic. Konrad Adenauer stayed there twenty-one times, followed by successive Chancellors. It was here, in a suite of apartments with its own private lift, that Adenauer prepared for the reconciliatory Franco-German meetings which resulted in the treaty of co-operation signed in 1963. On a personal level, Adenauer got on extremely well with General de Gaulle, and the Elysée was conveniently near for an informal visit.

As for gossip about the eccentricities of the rich and famous, there is not a great deal; the spirit of the *Bristol* appears to discourage newsworthy antics. Charles Trenet, "the singing fool", did indeed throw some saucers out the window one evening, and Julie Andrews used to take cushions from her

suite for her siestas between takes on the film set. And that's about all. In any case, the *Bristol*, always discreet, is not saying.

The present management zealously protects its clientele from idle curiosity or unwelcome attention from the news media. It may be, also, that the flaunting of luxury is out of fashion. Fewer tourists come today to this mythical place. It appears that the *Bristol* prefers to let the well-heeled multitudes and the over-excited rock stars go elsewhere, while it concentrates on the unobtrusive decision-makers of the world of high finance. And this policy has worked well. Americans, Japanese, Germans, in need of

Càsar Pinnaü, who designed yachts for Aristotle Onassis, created this swimming-pool. Set in solid teak, it calls to mind the prow of an ocean liner sailing towards the Sacré Coeur and the Paris sky-line. A charming trompe-l'oeil of the Eden Roc hotel on the Cap d'Antibes strengthens the illusion.

conference rooms, fax machines, secretarial services, and, with less time to spare for relaxation than in earlier years, in need of fitness clubs too, find all those things and more here under one roof. It is only by staying at the *Bristol* that you discover how extraordinarily efficient it is. For example : by some kind of radar, the staff know when a guest leaves his room, even if only for a few minutes, and when he returns, he finds it has been tidied. Every guest is addressed by name by all members of staff, and it is of course out of the question that any employee would ever appear in any way self-seeking.

To avoid the slightest risk of awkwardness, it is useful to bring a written recommendation on a first visit to the *Bristol*. This is a hotel to be savoured, like a rich dessert after a good meal. Speaking of meals, the food served from his ultra-modern kitchens by the head chef Emile Tabourdiau is beyond praise. Old hands remember the "Wednesdays at the *Bristol*", when Pierre Jammet set the cat among the pigeons of uninventive luxury hotel catering by offering every week a menu which he guaranteed would never be repeated. The cellars are among the Top Ten in France. You may sample there, for instance, a seventy-year-old cognac or a bottle of Réserve *Bristol* 1865 champagne, part of a treasure trove discovered at the time of the Liberation. Or you may prefer a rare Château Petrus 80, or a Mouton-Rothschild 1958. The choice is yours.

Other amenities at the *Bristol* are the parking lot with space for two hundred cars – not many ho-

tels in Paris can offer the like – a hairdressing salon for men and women, and that curious swimming-pool already mentioned, made of massive teak to the specifications of Càsar Pinnaü, the naval architect who designed yachts for Niarchos and Onassis.

We have lifted a corner of the veil to show something of the intimate luxury of the *Bristol*. For two hours every morning, its revolving doors stand motionless to be waxed and polished. For the rest of the day, they are in constant motion, indifferent to external crises, welcoming whatever the future may hold.

One of the marble bathrooms, recently restored.
The round magnifying mirror is another of Hippolyte Jammet's inventions.

THE CRILLON

Ambassador to the world

The history of the Crillon brings to mind Russian dolls, for this hotel nestles in the Place de la Concorde which nestles in the history of France.

The story begins in the eighteenth century. What is now the Place de la Concorde – possibly the most famous street location in the world – was then a rudimentary mall with a few patches of grass here and there, rutted by the tracks of carriage wheels. It was bordered to the east by a ditch running the length of the Tuileries; to the south by the Seine ; to the west by a semi-circular moat at the opening of avenue des Tuileries – now the Champs-Elysées ; and to the north by the market-gardens which separated it from the houses on the Faubourg Saint-Honoré. When Louis XV chose this place as appropriate for yet another symbolic manifestation of his majesty, he announced an ar-chitectural competition. In 1758, unimpressed by the entries, he asked his friend and official architect, Jacques-Ange Gabriel, to show what he could do. Gabriel designed twin colonnaded palaces, which took twenty-five years to complete.

Then the King commissioned an equestrian statue of himself from Bouchardon. This was erected in 1763 in front of the palaces, in the great open space to be called place Louis XV. Thirty years later, renamed Place de la Révolu-tion, it was to be the spot where Louis le Bien-Aimé's grandson Louis XVI and his queen went to the guillotine. Place de la Concorde in 1795 ; Place Louis XV again in 1814 ; Place Louis XVI in 1826 (this name is still legible on a corner-stone of the *Crillon*) ; Place de la Charte in 1830 ; finally back to Place de la Concorde in 1836.

*Preceding pages : the
impressive façade on
Place de la Concorde is
the work of the architect
Gabriel.
In medallion : statues of
Henri IV and of his friend
and comrade-in-arms,
the stalwart Crillon,
stand in the main hall.*

*Right : an incomparable
view of the Concorde and
the Palais Bourbon from
one of the terraces.
Note the magnificent
Corinthian pillars.*

The statue of Louis XV was pulled down during the Revolution by order of the Constituent Assembly, to be replaced by a statue of Liberty, itself later replaced by that curious monument, the Luxor Obelisk.

An extraordinary feat of transport brought this Egyptian obelisk up the Nile and across the Mediterranean as a gift to Charles X from the sultan Mehemet Ali. On the 26th of October 1836 a crowd of Parisians watched open-mouthed as it was put in place under the direction of the architect Lebas. It is over three thousand years old, stands twenty-three metres high, weighs two hundred and twenty tons, and is inscribed with a wealth of hieroglyphs. It is now a striking part of what may well be the most beautiful city perspective in the world – the ensemble formed by the Carrousel, the Champs Elysées, the Madeleine, the pont de la Concorde, and the Assemblée Nationale. The place de la Concorde is octagonal and covers eighty-four thousand square metres. It was conceived as a testimony to the greatness of France. One might take the fountains around the Obelisk as standing for the seas and rivers which form her boundaries ; or one might think of the abundant fertiity of the countryside. The statues by Cortot and Pradier on the perimeter are symbolic of the great regional capitals : Strasbourg, Rouen, Lille, Marseille, Bordeaux, Nantes, Lyon and Brest.

Views of the inner patio,
past and present.
This jewel of 18th century
architecture is bright with
sun-umbrellas in fine
weather.
Following pages :
the magnificent Eagles
salon, and a detail of
ceiling.

The vicissitudes of the past might be said to be reconciled here. But the echoes of history still sound : whether they come from the Champs Elysées, which has seen so many triumphal marches and funeral processions, so many festal celebrations and explosions of violence ; or whether they come from the Tuileries and the Louvre by way of the Orangerie and the Jeu de Paume.

The Place de la Concorde is the heart of Paris. There one cannot but be aware of the long past, as the year 2000 cuts challengingly across the line of sight. In spite of the enforced leisure imposed by frequent traffic-jams, Parisians may forget to admire the beauty of their

square, a city-scape without equal. Consider the prospect of the rue Royale with the twin buildings in the foreground and the Madeleine behind. Consider the perfect proportions of the two corner *pavillons*, pedimented and stepped in the Italian style. Consider to the right the handsome edifice which now houses the Ministry of Marine Affairs, and was once a storehouse for the royal furniture. And there it is, on the other side of the rue Royale : the hôtel de *Crillon*. The original building was completed in 1765 by the architect Louis-François Trouard, with a beautiful Roman façade designed by his master, the great Gabriel. Trouard built the house for his friend the duc d'Aumont, a man of excellent taste, so that when Aumont bequea-

thed the property to him, Trouart became the owner of a veritable treasury of exquisite sculptures and wood-carvings, many of them in the *salon des Aigles* with its superb ceiling, still there today.

The hôtel de *Crillon* entered history on the 6th of February 1778, when the First French-American treaty was signed there. The signatories were Benjamin Franklin and Arthur Lee for the thirteen American states, and Gérard Conrad for France. Ten years later the property was acquired by François-Félix-Dorothée Berton de Balbes, comte de *Crillon* and his wife Marie-Charlotte de Corbon. M. de *Crillon* was a descendant of that "trusty *Crillon*" who was comrade-in-arms of Henri IV. He fought in all his master's battles except the Battle of Arques, which caused the king to write to him thus : "My trusty *Crillon*, why the devil were you not at my side on Monday last, on the most glorious of all occasions ? I would you had been there". The king's words may be seen today inscribed in the entrance hall of the hotel. *Crillon*'s descendants were soldiers of distinction also and the name is held in great honour in Avignon, native town of the family.

The *Crillon*s paid three hundred thousand livres for the house which from then on bore their name. In 1789 the comte de *Crillon* was present at the meetings of the Estates General, where he allied himself with the Third Estate. But he was suspected of Royalist sympathies and his property was seized. The family emigrated to Spain and the house was let. After the Revolution, it was repossessed by its lawful ow-

ners, the *Crillon* and Polignac families, who used it for many years as a private residence. Repairs to the façade were carried out between 1894 and 1896, at which time it was classified as a historic building. Then the duchesse de Polignac, daughter of the marquis de *Crillon*, decided to sell.

In 1907 a commercial company bought the house and two adjoining properties in rue Boissy-d'Anglas. The plan was to build the most magnificent hotel in Paris, perhaps in Europe. The brief given to the architect, Walter Destailleurs, was to reconstruct the whole with an eye to its new function, but to retain the elaborate decorativeness of the original. Destailleurs designed a hotel which amply fulfilled both requirements – sumptuous comfort, palatial décor. A superb foyer replaced the vaulted passage which used to give access to the great courtyard; what were once stables and outhouses became elegant salons. The project was completed in 1909. On the 11th of March, the *Crillon* held its first gala dinner to mark the opening. The new hotel quickly won an international reputation.

In the context of the time, this opening was a significant event. Paris had lagged behind other great capital cities in establishing up-to-date luxury hotels. The situation changed rapidly at the turn of the century : the *Grand Hôtel* was renovated in 1904, the *Ritz* and the *Meurice* date from more or less the same period, and were soon to be followed by hotels on the Champs-Elysées. The spirit of competition took hold, as hotels vied with one another in the ef-

General Leclerc liberated the Crillon on 24th August 1944. After the war, the general always stayed at the Crillon when he was in Paris.

fort to be the greatest, the most splendid. The beneficiaries of the rivalry were wealthy travellers given to complaining of the backwardness of French hostelries. Now at last there was a decent place to stay in Paris.

In that gilded period between 1890 and 1914, cosmopolitan society discovered the pleasure of changing hotels according to the season – from Paris to Monte-Carlo, from Cannes to Biarritz, from Vienna to Marienbad. The *Crillon* had as many champions as had the *Ritz*. Then came the Great War ; the hotel was requisitioned and became the general headquarters first of the English, later of the Americans. It was already the abode of kings, princes, statesmen, diplomats : in 1919, at the end of the Great War, it became the base of the Conference which set up the League of Nations, forerunner of the United Nations. A plaque on the first floor recalls the event. Woodrow Wilson, the American President, added his signature to the visitors' book, where the first signature is that of Louis Berthou, who, as Président du Conseil, came to dine with his ministers on the 2nd of December 1913.

Since then, the *Crillon* has seen itself as having a quasi-official role to play. In a time of military missions, Allied conferences, peace plans, guests of the French Republic were often guests of the hotel. The proximity of the American Embassy was another factor. At the outbreak of war in 1939, the *Crillon* again became the headquarters of the Allied forces. In its historic rooms warious councils of war were held. But its strategic position meant that from 1940 to 1944 it felt the full force of the Occupation. Then on the 24th of August 1944, after a bombardment which severely damaged the façade, (an event recorded in René Clément's film "Paris brûle-t-il ?") the hotel was liberated by General Leclerc, and two hundred German officers were taken prisoner. (Until his death, General Leclerc always stayed at the *Crillon* when he came to Paris.) During the Liberation the hotel was the temporary residence of General Eisenhower and other Allied commanders, as well as diplomats from the State Department. In 1946, after extensive repairs, it opened its doors again to its customary clients.

We shall return later to the splendours of the Louis Quatorze décor in this hotel which is palace, museum and theatre. It has been the setting of so many dramas that to turn the pages of its treasured visitors' book is to turn certain pages of twentieth century civilization. During the Jazz Age – between the introduction of Prohibition in 1919 and the Wall Street crash in 1929 – the *Crillon* and its sister hotels had their first period of glory. This was the era of "An American in Paris". Ernest Hemingway (who alternated between the *Crillon* and the *Ritz*) used the *Crillon* bar as a setting in the plot of "The Sun Also Rises" – that part where Jake Barmes waits for Brett Ashley, who never turns up. Indeed the whole of that wild generation of American writers passed through the *Crillon* bar (then the largest in Europe). Faulkner, for instance, and Scott Fitzgerald. One evening,

Scott and Zelda, both rather drunk, made the hotel the winning-post in a race from the Obelisk, and caused such a furore that the police had to be called to restore order.

A great hotel is the scene of fascinating contrasts. While the life of irresponsible pleasure was running its course below, more serious games were being played out on upper floors of the *Crillon*. So many of the great came to stay there that one might be forgiven for asking, who didn't ? For instance : The Queen of the Netherlands (1912) ; the philanthropist Andrew Carnegie, founder of Carnegie Hall (1913) ; the King and Queen of Denmark and Theodore Roosevelt, President of the United States (1914) ; King George V of England (1915) ; General Pershing (1917) ; Marshal Joffre and Marshal Pétain (1917) ; Sir Winston Churchill and Woodrow Wilson, President of the United States (1918) ; Tyrone Power (1939) ; Charlie Chaplin (1954) ; the Japanese Emperor Hirohito, for whom Paris was the *Crillon* (1972) ; Sophia Loren (1979) ; Jackie Kennedy, Gregory Peck, David Niven and Yul Brynner (1980) ; Orson Welles and Malcolm Forbes, the newspaper magnate (1985) ; Queen Fabiola of Belgium (1985).

One could go on for ever. Richard Nixon came, as did the Shah of Iran, Javier Perez de Cuellar when he was Secretary-General of the United Nations, Haile Selassie, Emperor of

The handsome Crillon entrance, through which so many statesmen and other celebrities have passed.
Below : in the main salon, a remarkable elephant liqueur cabinet. This unique crystal and bronze piece was made by Baccarat for the Universal Exhibition of 1878.

Ethiopia, Eleanor Roosevelt, Foster Dulles, Mobutu, the comte de Paris, Nelson Mandela, Mohammed V and Hassan II, kings of Morocco.

There are stories, of course, about many of these illustrious guests. For example : when Hassan used to stay at the hotel as a child, the staff were instructed not to disturb the little prince when he played with his trains in the corridor. Charles Lindbergh, arriving from Le Bourget after his historic flight across the Atlantic, was so exhausted after the uproarious welcome from the crowd that he had to be helped to his room. The laundry staff have never forgotten how during a Summit meeting at the Trianon they had to take in the washing of all the delegations. As for the eccentric Maharajah of Baroda, his great terror was that he would be poisoned, so his personal cooks had always to be in attendance, even at the *Crillon*. One evening he arrived at a première in the Lido, complete with his own lamb and rice !

Such a clientele poses problems of protocol. When the Israeli Prime Minister, Yitzhak Shamir, came to Paris in 1988 for peace talks with his Egyptian opposite number, Moubarak, it was imperative to provide two suites of identical standing on different floors, and to guarantee that there could be no accidental encounters before the appointed time. As a result of its success in carrying out these conditions, the

Crillon is now always chosen for meetings in Paris of senior diplomats, ministers and heads of State from East and West. A related point : all the windows on the ground floor are bullet-proof.

It is worth noting that the hotel attracts politicians as well as the cream of the world of show-business and the arts. The *Crillon* is good at mixing different types of guest. Most of the great of our time from various backgrounds have chosen to come to this brilliant Paris grand-stand. Elizabeth Taylor, for example, is a regular occupant of one of the three Royal suites. The Blue suite, naturally always adorned with mauve-blue flowers, is named after her. She spent many happy hours there with Richard Burton.

Other signatures in the visitors' book are those of Madonna, Bette Davis, Jessie Norman, Charles Boyer, Gene Kelly, Meryl Streep, Woody Allen, Tom Cruise, Max Ernst, Richard Chamberlain, Robert Mitchum, Paloma Picasso, John Travolta. Above his autograph, Thierry Le Luron wrote : "This is the real *Crillon*". Serge Gainsbourg's contribution reads : "The Book is dreaming, don't disturb it". Further, the hotel provides a set film directors dream of; think, for instance, of "Rive droite, rive gauche", "American Dreamer", "Le Dernier Métro", "La Belle Histoire", among so many others. On at least one occasion, the décor of the *Crillon* was reproduced in a Hollywood studio, when Lubitch wanted it as a setting for "Ninotshka", that great classic of the cinema starring Greta Garbo.

Clients rarely come incognito. When they do, their wish for anonymity is scrupulously respected by the management. They will never reveal the identity of that American Croesus who asked to have the walls of his suite hung all over with gold and silver balloons for his wedding anniversary. The balloons all ended up on the ceiling, in a tangle reminiscent of a Douannier Rousseau jungle. Nor will they name the Arab potentate whose entourage demanded that, overnight, one star should be sawed off the star-shaped key-rings to obliterate any hint of the Star of David !

If you should venture to taste for once in your life the heady delights of staying at the *Crillon*,

Left ; one of the earliest official delegations from the Republic of China, June 1914.
Opposite : the main staircase and one of the marble bathrooms.
Below : a luxurious double bedroom.

waited on like a king, you might try, for instance, the suite the conductor Leonard Bernstein was so fond of, and which bears his name. It has been recently renovated and boasts a beautiful Italian terrace with a panoramic view over Place de la Concorde and the gardens of avenue Gabriel. If your are lucky, you may catch sight of the Eiffel Tower and the Arc de Triomphe floating on the horizon against the setting sun.

The hundred and sixty-three bedrooms and suites are all sound-proofed; all the beds are decked in silk and satin. Some manage to give a sense of privacy in the midst of splendour. That is not quite the effect of the three Royal or Presidential suites on the third floor – the Blue (Elizabeth Taylor) ; the White (Michael Jackson) ; the Red (Julia Migenes). These are known as *les grands appartements*. But the real trump cards held by the *Crillon* are on the first floor; there, you might believe yourelf to have been transported to Versailles. The three great reception rooms – *le salon des Aigles, le salon des Batailles, le salon de Marie-Antoinette* – can be turned into private apartments for official guests by opening adjoining rooms to serve as bedrooms.

The *salon des Aigles* possesses a magnificent Hungarian parquet floor, Aubusson carpets, Bohemian crystal, *alto-relievo* sculpture, gold-leaf decoration and wonderful Wedgwood china. (Wedgwood was one of the great English potters of the 18th century, some of whose work is on display in the museum at Sèvres. Wedgwood designers looked to antiquity for their inspiration.) But what have eagles to do with this salon ? Lift your eyes to the ceiling. Around the soberly plain centre you will see at each of the four corners two eagles with outstretched wings, surrounded by a design of flowers and ancient helmets. Four medallions represent Strength, Truth, Wisdom and Plenty. This is the room where from February to April 1919 the historic sessions took place which led to the setting up of the League of Nations.

In the *salon Marie-Antoinette*, the Flanders tapestry "The Singing Lesson" suggests that the Queen might have tried to learn to sing without notable success. Nowadays the salon is used for receptions which sometimes spill over on to the

Opposite and left : Marie Antoinette salon. Terrace on Place de la Concorde with marble statue. Below : The Blue suite, always Elizabeth Taylor's favourite.

terrace with its Corinthian columns overlooking the Concorde.

The *salon des Batailles* also looks out on the Concorde. It is so called because of the two paintings that hang there. This grey, gold and white room has Louis Seize furniture, fine wood-carving, and a magnificent coffered ceiling.

A great hotel which is also an historic building demands constant maintenance which is sensitive to its past, demands architects of high talent who are alert to the special responsibilities of their task. Since 1981 the *Crillon* has been engaged in a number of renovation schemes under the direction of Jean-Loup Robert, winner of the Grand Prix de Rome, chief architect at the Opera and the Grand Palais. Four hundred million francs have been invested in the work. Thanks to the fashion designer and interior decorator Sonia Rykiel, the hotel is a place for living as well as a museum. The harmony has been achieved by taking into account both the recommendations of the Historic Buildings Commission and the requirements of a modern luxury hotel.

The salon which was once the private chapel of Marie-Louise de *Crillon* is a case in point. The 18th century wood-work, like the painted panelling throughout the hotel (the Hirohito room is a fine specimen), has been faithfully restored by master craftsmen, specialists in the gold-leaf work in Versailles. There is in the Metropolitan Museum in New York a full-scale replica of one of the classified bedrooms at the *Crillon*.

A show-piece of which the hotel is justly proud is *Les Ambassadeurs*, the restaurant which fronts on the Place de la Concorde. Here there is marble on all sides, as in the *salon Gabriel*, in frequent demand for congresses and seminars, and in many other salons. But *Les Ambassadeurs* has something special to offer — the delight of watching the spectacle reflected in the glass of doors and mirrors. A gleaming dance of crystal chandeliers and attendants in formal dress whirls and shimmers, vanishes and reappears, in subtle, ever-changing pa-terns.

Around the ceiling of this hall of mirrors, frescoes by the painter Moreau-Néret represent

tings of Lalique glass. There is a new bar designed by Sonia Rykiel, with mosaics by the sculptor César.

Like *Les Ambassadeurs*, the *salon d'Honneur* has also a glass and marble décor. It opens on an 18th century courtyard which is embellished in fine weather with flowers and sun-umbrellas. This salon serves as a tea-room where a harpist or pianist may be playing. It boasts a fascinating centre-piece : a liqueur cabinet in the shape of an elephant. This rare piece of Baccarat crystal was created for the *Exposition universelle* of 1878. It was inspired by the "elephant of the Bastille", the fountain which the architect Alavoine designed for Napoleon the First, and which was never constructed.

Times have changed, however, at the *Crillon* as elsewhere. Nowadays there are no permanent residents. The last client to make a home in the hotel was the grand-daughter of Alexander Fleming, the man who discovered penicillin. (She lived there for thirty years, her only outings daily visits to the pigeons in the Tuileries gardens.) Yet this refuge of the last millionaires

the building being constructed by cherubs. The fantasy is pushed to the limit, with every monument in the Concorde included in the design. *Les Ambassadeurs* is a place of the highest tone where ritual is flawlessly performed. There is not a single false note ; every meal is a symphony of the table. In a second restaurant, *L'Obélisque*, which specializes in traditional French food, diners may admire the light fit-

still provides in its forecourt a continuous ballet of chauffeur-driven limousines, for it specializes in accommodating top-level companies for their seminars and business meetings.

The *Crillon* has one essential qualification to be regarded as a symbol of the art of French hotel-keeping : it is the only hotel of its class in Paris which is completely French-owned. The establishment is French through and through. It is also entirely up-to-date, always ready to move with the times. For instance, in what was once the guard-room, there is a boutique offering a range of more than two hundred luxury items, all from top designers ; leather goods, peignoirs, fashion accessories of various kinds are the most popular lines.

M.Jean Taittinger, president of the Société du Louvre which controls the hotel and its sister establishments in the Concorde group, is no doubt correct in seeing his *Crillon* as a most eloquent ambassador for France and the French art of graceful living. We may add : does anyone wish to live in a historic monument ? Yes ! Provided we are granted the privilege of

doing so here in the brilliance of the Concorde and of history.

At the *Crillon*, everyone is a king.

The famous visitors' book at the Crillon has a most impressive guest-list. Shown here, record of Boris Yeltsin's visit after he became Russian leader.

THE GEORGE V

America in the Paris edition

The *George-V*, work of the architects Lefranc and Wybo, may bear the name of an English king, but the style of decoration and of welcome is distinctively French.

The hotel is nine storeys high, built around three sides of an inner courtyard. The façade fronts on to avenue George-V, and has two projecting sections which run back into the building to form two sides of the garden or patio within. Between these two sections is the portico where guests enter the hotel under three large arcades leading into the reception hall. This central section consists of only one storey and has an enormous flat roof.

The upper storeys – those above the pediment dividing the fourth and fifth floors – are stepped in such a way that the patio and all the bedrooms and suites get full sun. The wing built in 1931 which gives on to avenue Pierre 1er de Serbie has a stepped structure also. This wing was for years a block of apartments, which could be rented by the season or by the year, for long-term letting, the residents having the right to use all the amenities of the hotel proper.

The architecture of the façade is neo-classical in spirit and in style, its symmetry emphasized by the two curved pediments at fifth floor level, and in particular by the squared pediments on the double Tuscan pillars in the upper loggias.

The inner or marble courtyard, as it is called, was originally designed simply to give pleasure to the eye. From their windows guests could enjoy the prospect of a charming formal garden with a fountain and box hedges and winding

Preceding pages : gourmet
restaurant, trompe-l'oeil
décor.
In medallion : pictorial
version of the hotel's logo.

Right : the Renaissance
fireplace in this salon
came from a château on
the Loire.
On the overmantel,
Aubusson tapestry with
French coat of arms early
in Louis XIV's reign.

shrubs, lawns and immaculate gravelled walks –
the whole immaculately kept. Nowadays it is
used as a summer restaurant.

The *George-V* has always been popular with
American visitors. They like it partly because of
its ideal situation in the very heart of Paris, and
partly because of descriptions like this in American newspapers : "elegant, luxurious, fully
up-to-date, incorporating the latest developments in hotel comfort, bringing to mind our
American hotels which influenced its design".

Attention to the convenience of clients has
always been a priority. In the thirties, guests
used to be met at Cherbourg or Le Havre, a ser-

or Le Touquet, for example, or to one of the golf-courses around Paris. In the inter-war years, the *George-V* was already leading the field in its use of new technology. You could have a "Meal-Recording" as today you can have a video-recording of a meeting. What happened was that a device was placed under the table, so that guests could have a recording of a luncheon or dinner engagement.

Since its establishment in 1928, the *George-V* has been a favourite choice of the stars : Greta Garbo, Terence Young, Gene Kelly, Buster Keaton, Cecil B. de Mille, Duke Ellington, Bob Dylan, Burt Lancaster, Jean Gabin, Marlene Dietrich, Vittorio da Sica, Sophia Loren, Dietrich Fischer Diskau, Sidney Poitier and the Rolling Stones among others. It has of course always attracted millionaires from various parts of the world, principally from America. And it seems that Georges Simenon knew it well enough to use it as a setting for one of his novels, "Maigret voyage". But the *George-V* has also been the setting for more serious events.

In February 1929, the Commission for War Reparations met there, with Owen D.Young as president and the American banker J.Pierpoint Morgan one of its members. The place was a sort of branch of the League of Nations at that period. On the 30th of October 1930 the hotel welcomed the French airmen Coste and Bellonte after their first non-stop transatlantic crossing from Dallas *via* New York to Paris. A rather different project came to fruition in the

Above : the Regency suite and its oak panelling.
Following pages : left, the George V about 1935, receptionists and porters under the entrance portico.
Below : photo taken from top floor terrace shows a fine private house, now demolished, opposite the hotel.
Right : a quiet corner of the galerie de la Paix, which takes its name from the fine 17th century Flemish tapestry by Leyniers, "Peace leading Plenty".

vice which made sense, considering that 60% of these were Americans and 30% English. In April 1930, the hotel introduced an air-taxi service with Farman aircraft, linking Le Bourget to London, Berlin and Madrid. Fares were from 3,600 to 6,000 francs. There was also a three-seater B.B Nieuport available for short trips to places not easily reached by road – to Deauville

salon Young where the statutes of the International Bank at Basle were drawn up. And in 1944, after the liberation of Paris, General Eisenhower made the hotel his temporary base before moving to the *Trianon Palace*.

The *George-V* has always made the improvement of standards of luxury and comfort its goal, a goal realized in the bedrooms and suites (currently standing at three hundred and ten) as much as in the salons, galleries, dining-rooms and reception areas. Throughout the hotel numerous works of art of the highest quality collected by the Dupré family are shown to advantage in a dazzling architectural setting. Between 1989 and 1992, two hundred million francs were spent on a complete renovation of the building, inside and out.

Apartment with four-poster bed. Every suite is richly furnished with 17th and 18th century pieces: chests, wardrobes, tables, sculptures and pictures.

The entrance hall was restored in 1990 by the architect Alain Mertens. Behind the semi-circular reception desk hangs a seventeenth-century Brussels tapestry depicting the Victory of Ceres (Roman goddess of the harvest). The two French windows boast the elaborate metal tracery typical of the thirties. The Savonnerie carpet is an exact reproduction of a carpet in the *Mobilier national*.

If you stroll through the corridors and if you explore the various salons of the hotel, you will discover an impressive collection of *objets d'art* and antiques. In the *salon bleu* there is a bust of the duchesse de Chaulnes by Frattinet and a bronze by Delamare of Adam and Eve disporting themselves among the animals in the garden of Eden. In the corridor to the right stands a bust of Mansart by Coysevox.

The *Galerie de la Paix* gets its name from its 17th century Flemish tapestry made from cartoons by Leyniers and depicting Peace leading Plenty by the hand. There is also a fine Regency time-piece in this gallery.

The *salon de l'Horloge* gets its name from the huge wall-clock, a rare piece in carved polychrome wood in Louis Quatorze style. This room contains another Flemish tapestry by Leyniers, in this case a representation of the Evils of War. The octagonal *salon Régence* has the basin of a terracotta fountain from the château of Pontchartrain, property during the Second Empire of the famous marquise de Païva. The Regency panelling came from a château in Normandy. On the walls are 17th and 18th century tapestries and carpets from Aubusson, Flanders and Beauvais. One beautiful piece in this room is a still life by Boschenis.

The *salon Louis XIII* is remarkable for its fine carved wood and for a magnificent Renaissance fire-place in carved stone from a château mear Sully-sur-Loire. Above the mantel-piece there is an Aubusson tapestry from the "Chancellors" series which shows the Royal coat-of-arms at the beginning of the reign of Louis XIV. There are other beautiful objects to admire in this salon :

the Louis Treize furniture, a Beauvais tapestry made in 1724, a 15th century wood-carving representing John the Evangelist.

In the *salon Napoléon* there are fascinating early 19th century bronze flambeaux : each represents a female figure holding on her head a seven-branched candelabrum.

The *salon d'Auteuil* is embellished by two magnificent Napoleon III chandeliers and pale grey marble pillars. The double doors of the *salon Vendôme* open on to a room containing caryatids in wood and pillars in blue-grey marble.

The charming *salon Chantilly* has a painted ceiling with a floral motif in Renaissance style. The walls are decorated with *trompe-l'œil* scenes from the gardens at Versailles.

The gourmet restaurant *Les Princes* was founded by André Sonier in the seventies. It is a place of tall arcades and pillars painted in *trompe-l'œil*.

The credit for these treasures of art and architecture goes to two men – Sir Charles Forte and André Sonier. During the seventies, André

Opposite : detail of recently decorated bedroom.
Below : Greta Garbo, a regular client at the George V, on a Hollywood set for the film "Grand Hotel".
Righthand page : staircase leading to a salon, with imitation marble stucco pillars.

Sonier took steps to make the *George-V* one of the most exciting luxury hotels in Paris : a year-long Utrillo exhibition in the restaurant *Les Princes* ; the organization of important fine-art auctions and of the antique dealers' Biennale ; the opening of luxury boutiques, of Broom's club, of a centre in the hotel cellars for the sampling and sale of rare wines. In 1978, there was a spectacular celebration of the fiftieth anniversary of the hotel, one of the high points of which was an "April in Paris" ball. For this glittering occasion, 600 guests (including 150 American millionaires) were brought by special plane to spend a long week-end in Paris.

Through all these initiatives, the *George-V*, in the decade 1970 to 1980, has increased its profits and the number of guests it receives. Today, it is again that "sleek transatlantic place in the most aristocratic avenue in Paris", as the poet Léon-Paul Fargue put it.

Allegorical figure in recess, one of the many sculptures in the George V collection. Few hotels can boast of a richer collection of period pieces. Opposite page : the aviator Coste. He stayed at the George V in October 1930, after his first transatlantic flight with Bellonte.

THE GRAND HOTEL

Second Empire flamboyance

When the *Grand Hotel* was built in 1862, the Opéra was still only at the foundations stage. But the architect of the hotel, Alfred Armand, had to ensure that his plan was in keeping with the projected monument and with the new layout of streets and squares Haussmann was creating for the Paris of the Second Empire.

The *Grand Hotel* was built with remarkable speed. It took only fifteen months. This feat was achieved by superb planning. The contributions of the range of tradesmen involved were perfectly coordinated ; every job had its precise place in the over-all work schedule. The stone slabs for the façade arrived from the Saint-Maximim quarries already cut and numbered according to their eventual position. Arc lamps were used so that work could continue uninterrupted day and night – an innovation which made exciting copy for the newspapers of the time.

The opening ceremony of the *Grand Hôtel de la Paix* took place on the 5th of May 1862 in the presence of the Empress Eugénie. Madame Patti and Madame Piccolomini sang an extract from "La Traviata". Jacques Offenbach and Olivier Métra conducted the orchestra. An act from a play by Labiche – "Vingt-neuf degrés à l'ombre" – was performed. The evening was rounded off by a ball attended by everybody who was anybody in Paris.

The building has the splendour of a monument, with its echoing pattern of pilasters and cornices, balustrades and pediments, wrought-iron balconies and zinc-faced mansard upper storeys.

Some facts and figures: it had been intended that "the biggest caravanserai in the world" should have a thousand bedrooms; in the event these were limited to eight hundred. The ground area is 8 000 square metres; the total floor area comes to over seven hectares. The perimeter of the four façades, Capucines Scribe-Auber-Opéra, measures 500 metres. There are 440 windows on each storey, which makes 2 200, plus another 1 000 giving on to the inner court-yards.

Up to 1914 the banquet-hall doubled as the hotel dining-room; it could seat 600 guests. It

Ionic pillars are set with mirrors in which the movement of the brilliant scene, lit by chandeliers and flambeaux, is endlessly reflected. At second-floor level, there are forty-eight pillars representing female figures, two for each of the twenty-four concave arches. These caryatids depict musicians playing various instruments – cymbals, castanets, triangles, lyres, pipes of Pan and so forth.

Above the architraves with their scroll-work decoration the ceiling converges towards the central glass lantern, seven metres in diameter. Another striking feature of the *salon Opéra* is the remarkable fireplace embellished by a clock-face and two statues by Klogmann representing Love.

A feature of the *Grand Hotel* in the 19th century was a billiard room with ten tables and, from 1880 on, a full-time instructor. One historic match in February 1882 went on for a week. The contestants were the French champion François Vignaux and the American Slosson. The boulevard and the square were crowded throughout the match by fans eager to read the latest scores as they were posted on a notice-board outside the hotel.

In the nineties the *Compagnie des Wagons-Lits* established an agency in che hotel. There was also a news room displaying the latest prices on the Stock Exchange, the departure-times of boats and other such up-to-the-minute information.

At a time when horse-racing was all the rage – when Chantilly, Longchamp and Auteuil dictated the fashion in hats – the *Grand Hotel* was the place to go for a vehicle to take you to the race-course. "Le Figaro" had this to say : "The most Parisian place in Paris is the *Grand Hotel*. There, particularly in the week before the Grand Prix, one may observe the cosmopolitan scene in all its splendour". It offered race-goers their choice of livery coaches, coupés, victorias, landaus...even of bicycles from 1901 on. It must be admitted that the last-named mode of transport did not catch on !

There is another amenity of the hotel in its early days which is worth recording. Between 1862 and 1880 the after-dinner concerts at the hotel were a very popular attraction. These

was renamed the *salon Opéra*, in honour of Charles Garnier, a frequent diner in his neighbourhood restaurant. Today it is one of the grandest hotel salons in Paris. Semi-circular in shape, it rises thirty metres in height, the height of three storeys. At ground-floor and first-floor level, the arcades with their elaborately worked

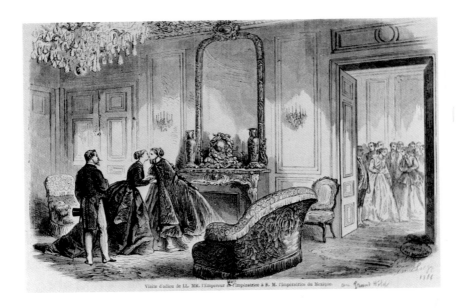

was as famous as, say, the cellar of the *Taillevent* restaurant is today. All of the great French wines and spirits were stocked in its three cellars which between them had a capacity of 400 000 bottles. The cellar used to be chiefly maintained by the *café de la Paix*, then a more or less automonous enterprise before it was taken over in 1898 by Arthur Millon, one of the principal shareholders of the hotel.

A striking feature of the amenities provided by the *Grand Hotel* was the bathing complex in the mezzanine. There were fifteen bathrooms, turkish baths, rooms for hydrotherapy and massage as well as a hair-dressing salon. Toda these services are located on the top floor of the Opéra wing.

The best apartments were those on the first floors of the Opéra and Capucines wings. All these apartments had fireplaces and each one was embellished with ornamental moulding, carved wood panelling, mirrors, paintings, medallions, carpets and reproduction furniture in Louis Quinze, Louis Seize and Empire styles. Rooms were priced according to the floor they were on, a detail Zola uses in "Nana" : "Higher up, on the fourth floor, the price was twelve francs. Rose, wanting something fitting but unostentatious, decided on a room with mahogany furniture, Louis Treize cretonne with a design of huge flowers, and a red carpet with a black leaf pattern".

Towards the end of the century, upholstered comfort typical of the Second Empire yielded to new notions of hygiene. Under the influence of César Ritz, all bedrooms were gradually equipped with private bathrooms and the general décor became less elaborate.

In the early 1900s travel guides used to exhort their readers to be discriminating in their choice of hotel. Any hotel would not do for people of taste. They should consider what was due to their position in the world. In short, the only fitting place for a successful man and his high-toned family was a hotel of the highest class.

The success of the *Grand Hotel* depended in the main on a middle class clientele. This kind of visitor liked the package it offered – lodging,

were held in the banquet hall and drew large audiences.

From the start, as well as the *table d'hôte* dining-room, there was another smaller, more intimate restaurant with an excellent gourmet bill of fare. This stood on the site of the present bar – to the right of the *cour d'honneur*, near the *café de la Paix*. It started as an after-the-show restaurant. Later it served mid-day as well as evening meals. The wine-cellar of the *Grand Hotel* was reputed for the excellence and range of its wine-list, and for more than fifty years supplied non-residents as well as hotel guests. It

The glass roof designed for the main courtyard by Henri Nénot was removed in the 1960s. A less elaborate version has recently been installed over the gourmet restaurant.

*Suite at the Grand Hotel.
Opposite page, top :
a fan dating from
the opening of the winter
garden in 1906.
Below, apartment on two
levels and private
sittingroom. The layout of all
bedrooms and apartments
has been completely
redesigned in recent years.*

*Double page following :
the original ballroom, now
the Opera salon, one of the
largest reception rooms in
Paris. It is a classified
monument for its superb
Second Empire décor,
recently restored. Note the
admirable proportions of its
three storeys, 30 metres in
diameter, and above the
bays, the forty-eight
caryatids representing
musicians.*

meals and bright lights all included. And they felt flattered by rubbing shoulders with such celebrities as favoured the hotel with their presence.

So wide was the range of services on offer that guests might well feel they were living like princes. Travel agency, restaurants, pharmacy, post-office, tobacconist (with the best stock of Havanas in Paris), doctor, dentist, dressmakers, florists, photographer. The last mentioned was Nadar, from 1893 the foremost night-photographer. His premises were opposite the hotel in boulevard des Capucines. Guests could have meals brought to their rooms at any time they chose. Even the milk was exceptional, co-

ming as it did from the Swiss herd on the hotel's own farm on the outskirts of Paris.

A number of royal personages used the *Grand Hotel* as a temporary residence. One of these was the Empress Charlotte, wife of Maxmilian, Emperor of Mexico. Empress Eugénie came to visit her there.

Pashas from the Far and Middle East, Brazilian and other Latin-American potentates, Russian princes, maharajahs, reigning monarchs such as the Shah of Persia, or their spouses, the Queen of Portugal, for example : with visitors like these to spread the fame of its excellence and elegance, it is not surprising that the hotel acquired a world-wide reputation.

There were also top civil servants, army officers, diplomats, politicians, industrialists, financiers. The average length of stay for most guests was five nights. Up to the turn of the century the notion of taking an apartment by the year had not yet come in.

Flamboyance, size, number of rooms, richness of décor were the hotel's characteristics. No less characteristic was the high level of comfort provided.

The hotel was quick to take advantage of technical advances at the end of the 19th century and led the way in installing the latest inventions – central heating, electric lighting and so on.

From the start, there was a residents' lift and a luggage-lift, both hydraulically operated. In the hotel's publicity brochures guests were reminded that the lift could be used for coming down as well as going up ! The lift was lavishly decorated. It looked rather like a miniature drawing-room. It was an object to be visited, one of the wonders of the place. In 1903 yet another sign of modern comfort appeared in the bedrooms – house telephones to replace the service bells. In 1911 all the rooms were connected to outside lines. Up to 1900, heating was provided by open fires and solid-fuel stoves. Then central heating was installed and there was an

Place de l'Opéra and Café de la Paix in 1935. Advertisement poster from 1900. By then, the Grand Hotel in Paris was well known all over the world.

Yves Montand in "Ça, c'est Paris", broadcast live from the Café de la Paix in 1947.

l'Opéra. The press gave the innovation a rapturous welcome, likening it to a private supper-room of the most elegant kind. At the end of the thirties, this bar was replaced by the *Pam-Pam*, a place for quick meals, forerunner of the present-day snack bar. The closing of the *Pam-Pam* in 1974 was to the advantage of the *foyer-bar Opéra* in the *café de la Paix*.

Two other popular features of the *Grand Hotel* were the Japanese bar, opened in 1896, and the grill-room, opened in 1898.

A spectacular innovation at the turn of the century was the winter garden, created by Henri Nenot, the architect who designed the new Sorbonne. The main entrance of the hotel was moved to its present position in rue Scribe, and the *cour d'honneur* was completely transformed. The winter garden was opened in 1907. Up to the thirties the tea-room equalled that of the *Ritz* in popularity. This impressive room measured twenty-three metres long by twenty-three metres wide and had a superb stained-glass roof.

The architecture of the *café de la Paix* (classified a historic building in 1972), is most stylish in effect with its pillars and painted ceiling. The terrace on the boulevard was added in 1862. Its popularity continues undiminished. Generations of visitors and celebrities have come from all over the world to see and be seen on this famous terrace.

When the CIGA group bought the *Grand Hotel* in 1974 the *café de la Paix* underwent a complete restoration. A veranda roof was installed above the terrace. Inside, its period splendour was recreated with scrupulous attention to every detail of gilding, murals, cherubs. This

end to the ritual of carrying fuel and hot water to the suites. Even after there was gas and later electric lighting in the public rooms, the bedrooms were still lit by oil lamps and candles up to 1896.

1894 saw the opening of the American bar, the first in Paris. Access was by way of place de

salon *Opéra* recovered its former splendour at the hands of a team of highly skilled craftsmen — painters, sculptors, specialists in plaster-work, gilding, bronze-work.

So when the *Grand Hotel* celebrated its hundred and thirtieth anniversary in June 1992, with Thomas Crowley, director-general of the group, and Madame Tsutsumi as principal guests of honour, it did so in a setting and with a panache worthy of the palmy days of the Second Empire.

Detail of Second Empire décor from one of the salons in the Café de la Paix, entered in 1974 in the Inventory of Historic Monuments for its architectural interest and its place in the history of Paris.

The bar in the Opéra restaurant, recently installed on the side of the hotel facing onto the rue Auber and the Opera House.

was also the time when the gourmet *restaurant Opéra* and the bar were established opposite place de l'Opéra.

Further major renovations followed after the hotel was taken over by an intercontinental corporation. (It is now a member of the Japanese group Seibu-Saison belonging to the illustrious Tsutsumi family.) Over five years at a cost of four hundred million francs a number of restoration projects have been carried out. The arcatures and painted ceiling of the boulevard des Capucines entrance have been restored ; a glass pyramid has been put back in place over the original *cour d'honneur* ; some anachronistic additions made during the sixties have been removed ; the main entrance hall and the reception area have been redecorated in a manner which celebrates the history of the place. In 1991 the

Type des Voitures de livraisons du Gᵈ Hôtel de Paris

Above, left : Ali, coffee maker extraordinary, symbolic of the Café de la Paix, where he officiated in the 1960s.
Above, right : the cellars of the Grand Hotel, with 400.000 bottles, were the largest in Paris up till 1914.

L'HOTEL

An adorable corner

To explore great hotels is, like Christopher Columbus, to come upon an exotic world. Whether you like it or not, you are an intruder, slipping into other people's lives to investigate the pleasures of seeing and being seen in a gilded salon. You pass through famous portals in the wake of famous guests. Which, you wonder, first confers the fame – the place or those who choose it ? What, for instance, makes the *Danieli* in Venise famous ? How much does it owe to the glamour surrounding it as the romantic setting for the love-affair between George Sand and Alfred de Musset ? In any case, it is certain that great hotels, even the most splendid, owe part of their reputation to celebrities who have frequented them.

So we put down our suitcases in all innocence on the spot trodden by Marcel Proust, André Gide, Rudyard Kipling, Graham Greene, Somerset Maugham or Ernest Hemingway. We can hardly say it's because there's a shortage of space ! But we would be intimidated if we stopped to think of those who have stood there before us, of how much talent and genius the walls of these hotels have seen. We enter what seems to be merely an empty bedroom, without pausing to wonder what destinies have been decided here, what passions, joys and griefs it has witnessed. If we were to allow ourselves to think of all the dramatic scenes enacted there, we would think it a sacrilege even to sit on the bed !

Do we really dare sleep in the bed where Elizabeth Taylor or Ava Gardner has slept ? The scene is set for the next act : the furniture smells of beeswax ; the covers have been meticulously turned back ; there is a pile of luxurious towels in the bathroom. Let us ask the

Preceding pages : the Mistinguett room and a portrait of Oscar Wilde. Right : Barbra Streisand.

Above : the unique circular courtyard, designed by the American architect Robin Westbrook with all the bedrooms situated around it in ancient Roman fashion.

genius of the place to allow us to absorb the atmosphere of the silent room. The French writer, Xavier de Maistre, has described the satisfaction of making a journey around one's own room. He did not add that the practice is not exactly restful.

The place we have reached on our journey through the world of the great hotels is a good example of ground covered by many illustrious travellers. Careful... Don't disturb the ghosts of

Oscar Wilde, of Mistinguett, of Jean-Gabriel Domergue. Odd that ghosts of such different natures should dwell together in the same lodging tucked away in a corner of Old Paris.

A word about the history of this ancient district. We are in the heart of Saint-Germain-des-Prés. Until the sixteenth century, this quarter was known as *Le Petit-Pré-aux-Clercs*. The "little meadow" was bordered on the north by quai Malaquais, on the east by rue Mazarine and rue de l'Ancienne-Comédie, on the west by rue Bonaparte and rue Saint-Benoît, and on the south by the abbey of Saint-Germain-des-Prés.

Much has been written about Saint-Germain-des-Prés, nowadays centre of the arts, haunt of young enthusiasms. There is no need to elaborate on the importance of the quarter in the life of literature, scholarship and art. What may be noted is that the place was predestined to yield a rich harvest. It began, in fact, as a great stretch of fertile park-land owned by the La Rochefoucauld-Liancourt family. Life always hummed about its central avenue, the present rue des Beaux-Arts, so named in 1824. We can go back farther still. The first ten even-numbered houses of the present rue des Beaux-Arts was the site of the palace of Queen Margot, who lived there until her death in 1615. Where N° 13 now stands, there used to be a charming country retreat, a *pavillon d'amour*, built over a beautifully proportioned set of cellars. The design is attributed to the architect Claude-Nicolas Ledoux.

Today in this fascinating street – the windows of the antique shops will certainly tempt you to linger – N° 13 is, appropriately enough, a darling of a hotel. A hotel which flaunts no name, is simply The Hotel. A hotel which subdues the conventional signs of its function and which combines the height of luxury with a touch of quaintness, irresistibly charming. Around 1815 – when the La Rochefoucauld-Liancourt family sold the park – the *pavillon* became a hostelry which gradually developed into a hotel. Six storeys were built around the original courtyard. It was first called *Hôtel d'Allemagne* ; in 1870 the name was changed to *Hôtel d'Alsace*.

Its beginnings were modest. The *Hôtel d'Alsace* attracted clients with very little cash to

One of the two suites (Robert de Niro always chose this one), with a view over the rooftops of St.Germain-des-Près.

spare. (That is no longer the case !) The owner-manager, M.Dupoirier, was a kind of universal uncle rather than a businessman. It was he who welcomed Oscar Wilde with open arms when Wilde fled to France after coming out of prison. He arrived in a wretched state. The *Hôtel d'Alsace* gave him kindly shelter and he stayed there until his death. He paid no bills and there was a large amount owing when he died – a circumstance that occasioned that last leap of wit : "I am dying beyond my means". There were no wreaths at his lonely funeral save one from M.Dupoirier : "In memory of my friend and guest".

At that time the hotel was still shabby ; its clients still short of money. Yet the street was moving up in the world, becoming a place where

distinguished men held court : at Nᵒ 3 the academicians Lacordaire and Montalembert ; at Nᵒ 4 the sculptor Pradier ; at Nᵒ 5 the writer Gérard de Nerval ; at Nᵒ 8 the painter Fantin-Latour ; at Nᵒ 10 successively the painter Corot, the novelist Mérimée, the historian and academician Fantin-Latour.

For half a century nothing changed at the *Hôtel d'Alsace*. Then the miracle happened. Edmond Dreyfus, the textile king, and Guy-Louis Duboucheron, artist-cum-fashion-model-cum-actor, fell in love with the place. An American architect, Robin Westbrook, waved his magic wand like the fairy godmother in the story and turned the pumpkin into a royal coach. He built a period-style inn with the rooms opening on to the original central courtyard.

The Oscar Wilde room, with some of the writer's furniture and personal belongings.
Right : a contemporary portrait of Wilde, one of the features of the room.

Guy-Louis Duboucheron turned out to be a born interior decorator. He designed twenty-five bedrooms and two suites, consulting in the process friends, people who had stayed at the hotel, and most of all his own highly original taste. His ambition was to create a luxury hotel of such quality as to disabuse Americans of the idea that in French hotels they don't understand how to make you comfortable. Thus was born *L'Hôtel*. Simply that : The Hotel ; no other identification would be needed. The tiny palace was the first to install air-conditioning. Other places might strive to be the greatest money-spinners. At N° 13 rue des Beaux-Arts the ambition was of a different order. The prime consideration was to be perfection. Today, it is almost always booked to capacity. Oscar Wilde's room has been scrupulously reproduced in the style of the late nineteenth century. It contains some of Wil-

de's manuscripts as well as a letter from the proprietor, M.Dupoirier, to M.Melmoth (Wilde's pseudonym in Paris), asking for settlement of a bill. The very last bill is there too : To medecines, 54.10. To meals from Little Sisters of the Poor, 20. To nurse-attendant, 20. To shroud, 12. To 42 candles, 12.60. A poignant document, translating the manner of the writer's death into items and prices. Today, it must be said, prices are a little higher than in Wilde's time.

Another room always booked six months in advance is the *Mistinguett*. It is so called, not because Mistinguett ever stayed there, but because its furniture in the heady Art Deco style of the twenties once belonged to her. An enormous raised bed, a desk, two armchairs, a sofa, a dressing-table – all aglitter with mirror glass

picked out in blue, white and red. The interior decorator Jean-Gabriel Domergue created them for the Dolly Sisters. Mistinguett bought the set in 1927 and installed it in her house at Bougival. The great bed is where she died. After her death, her sister-in-law, Fraisette Bourgeois, offered the pieces to the Musée d'Art moderne, but the curator thought them too cum-

Bill furnished to Oscar Wilde, left unpaid at his death. This bill, handwritten by the proprietor, is one of the mementos preserved at the hotel. Below : no two bedrooms have the same décor.

bersome and declined to accept the gift. Ed-mond Dreyfus (a friend of Mistinguett and of the Guitrys) and Guy-Louis Duboucheron seized the golden opportunity of creating a perfect living museum.

There are other fascinating rooms, each of which must have cost a small fortune. One has a leopard-skin motif throughout. In another, every piece of furniture is signed by the maker. Co-lour-schemes go from bright red through rose-pink to grass green. The charming bathrooms are done in Venetian marble. A feature of the hotel is that every room is quite different from all the others. Moreover, every room is a self-contained unit with its own tiny lobby, all of them soundproofed and equipped with every conceivable gadget. Even in the panelled corri-dors there is always something worthy of atten-tion – you may turn a corner and come upon ori-ginal drawings by Cocteau.

There was a time in the seventies when the hotel was over-full of such treasures, like the Toulouse-Lautrec pictures or the furniture that had belonged to Victor Hugo, so that there was perhaps a certain sense of being in a museum. This effect of heaviness has been lightened in re-cent years, but there is still a great deal of ex-quisite period furniture to enjoy, such as late eighteenth-century armchairs, bronze lamps and splendid lithographs.

At *L'Hôtel* you may, if you wish, try all the rooms in turn. Your things will be transferred for you. The change won't in the least perturb the staff. On the contrary, they wish only to gratify your slightest whim. This is, after all, The Hotel, where the service is unfailingly attentive and courteous. A staff member thinks nothing of

spending half-an-hour helping you to track down somebody who sells baby crocodiles. The exceptional friendliness between guests and staff shows itself even in the way the staff dress – not in uniform but in formal town wear. You are among gentlefolk.

The ambiance created suggests the easy in-teraction of a private club. There is too the sense that all the place has to offer is not on dis-play. There is always something more. So the ty-pical clientele of great hotels find their way here eventually, attracted by the atmosphere. Guy-Louis Duboucheron understood the importance of satisfying the desire for something out of the

If you would like to know who has slept in Mistinguett's bed or in Oscar Wilde's, you must consult a list as long as the list of present-day star celebrities : Ava Gardner, Lisa Minnelli, Nureyev, Mastroianni, the Rolling Stones, Monica Vitti, Roman Polanski, Leonor Fini, Marie Bell, Josephine Baker, princess Grace of Monaco, the Aga Khan, Johnny Hallyday, Jean Marais, Natalie Wood, Paul McCartney, Barbra Streisand. Kate Bush and all the American Top Fifty, the Argentinian writer Jorge Luis Borge – it is impossible to mention all who came here to dim the lustre of their names for a while in this romantic hotel which declines to take a name and which does not need to advertise.

Understandably, not many politicians stay here. But many American businessmen and oil-barons are drawn to the charms offered here on the Left Bank. Members of the French establishment make an occasional appearance, enjoying a little relaxation in a setting where a Feydeau farce would not be out of place. Other kinds of people come too.

The lunch-time guests tend to be more restrained, more preoccupied – writers and dealers in antiques ; top fashion-designers and their budding models.

The two present owners, Alain-Philippe Feutré and Guy-Louis Duboucheron, have brought it off : *L'Hôtel* is an exclusive residence of superb comfort and highly sophisticated taste, where a well-filled wallet is not in itself a sufficient qualification for admission.

ordinary. To occupy one of the two suites on the sixth floor (Robert de Niro's favourites) overlooking the church of Saint-Germain-des-Prés and the *Ecole des Beaux-Arts*, is to experience the delightful illusion that the whole district has taken you to its heart.

Throughout – in the foyer with its pouffes and semi-circular seats upholstered in red velvet, in the restaurant *Le Bélier* (so named in honour of Duboucheron's birth-sign Aries) in the vaulted sitting-rooms and dining-rooms (once the cellars) – Charles Trenet's sweet warblings ripple from the silk-covered walls and mingle with the rushing sound of the fountain in the courtyard.

THE INTER-CONTINENTAL

The Empress's palace

Every year on her way through Paris, the Empress Eugénie stayed at this hotel. She made her last visit in December 1919."

These words are engraved in gold lettering on a plaque to the left of the hotel entrance in rue de Castiglione. Eugénie de Montijo, one of its most renowned guests and one of the most faithful, usually stayed there from May to July over a period of more than twenty years. Perhaps she liked to relive past glories as she looked out at the Tuileries gardens nearby and the ruins of the palace which had been her home. Octave Aubry writes : "At the *Continental*, she always had the same apartment on the second floor. A bedroom, two sitting-rooms. [...] Not much room – or perhaps too much – for one who had been an Empress. She lifts the curtain. There, under her eyes, are the walks where she used to stroll with Louis-Napoleon, the gardens where their son used to play as a little boy".

At that time, Paris already had two luxury hotels : the *Louvre* and the *Grand Hotel*. The *Continental* opened its doors on the 6th of June 1878, the event timed to coincide with the third Exposition universelle.

In designing the front of the hotel, the architect Henri Blondel respected the sobriety so characteristic of all the buildings in rue de Rivoli and rue de Castiglione. His plan situated the whole of the new building around an immense *cour d'honneur* with a magnificent peristyle. (This courtyard is now a garden and summer restaurant.)

When you enter the *Inter-Continental*, as the hotel is now called, you first pass two great

Preceding pages : at the hotel entrance, two bronze candelabra from a palace in Saint Petersburg.
Medallion shows portrait of Empress Eugénie de Montijo.
As an official at Foreign Affairs in the 1940s, Jean Giraudoux had an office at the Continental.
Right : detail of a Delaplanche sculpture on the fireplace in the Imperial salon.
Below : the old Moorish salon, now demolished, looked on to the summer garden courtyard.
A journalist of the time called it " a corner of the Alhambra wafted to Paris by a magic wand".

bronze statues by Coutan representing Music, you go round by the right of the patio to the lobby, a comfortably welcoming place, where you may very well find a charming lady harpist playing music by Eric Satie. Then you come to the reception desk. This unusual arrangement, quite exceptional in the great Paris hotels, gives the guest time to get the feel of the place before picking up his key from the receptionist.

The most prestigious of the hotel's four wings overlooks the arcades in rue de Rivoli, opposite the Tuileries gardens. In the café-restaurant on this side – the *Tuileries* – you can hear an excellent jazz pianist every evening. The most exclusive suites are on the first floor of the same wing.

The magnificent public rooms at the *Inter-Continental* bear comparison with the foyer of the

The Imperial suite, overlooking rue de Rivoli and the Tuileries gardens, honours the memory of Empress Eugénie. Great fireplace in the Imperial suite: detail of flambeaux.

Opéra. The numerous paintings and sculptures are worthy reminders of the talents of their creators : Laugée, Faustin-Besson, Mazerolles, Delaplanche. The grandeur of these compositions, covering the ceilings and upper cornices, is continued in a wealth of copper-studded panelling in ebony and other rare woods, impressive pillars and chandeliers, monumental fireplaces, all executed in Louis Quatorze and Louis Quinze styles. The overall effect is truly that of a royal residence.

General view of the huge Imperial salon. Its décor, in the eclectic style typical of the late 19th century, has earned it inclusion in the Inventory of Historic Monuments.
Detail of cornice and lintel of fireplace, and detail of vase-shaped face of the astronomical clock. Sculptures by Delaplanche.

Several of the public rooms, all available for cocktail parties, lectures and conferences, are so wonderfully decorated that they have earned the hotel a place in the list of historic buildings.

The *salon Napoléon*, reached from the covered passage around the courtyard, is a huge room of 220 square metres. Pale Corinthian columns with gold-leaf work on their capitals support the wide ceiling cornices. The ceiling is coffered, each of its three sections surrounded by gilded mouldings and arabesques. Over each door there is a design of floral motifs. The central panel of the ceiling is an allegorical painting by Joseph Mazerolles, representing Jupiter and Mercury. Over the white marble fireplaces mirror-glass panels are ornamented by busts of children.

The *salon impérial*, measuring 29 by 13 metres, is the largest room in the hotel. The fluted Corinthian columns and the pilasters framing the high windows on the two longer sides support a great entablature above which the sectioned arches are decorated with frescos depicting mythological subjects and floral motifs. The ceiling is in three sections divided by rich gilded mouldings and escutcheons in high relief. The frescos were painted by Laugée in 1879, some considerable time therefore after the official opening of the hotel.

The theme chosen for the four lateral panels is the Four Seasons. In the central panel and the two round panels of the ceiling itself, the

themes are the Triumph of Love, Dawn, and Night.

These panels are separated by vases of flowers sculpted in high relief. In the centre and in the corners seated female figures represent the liberal arts.

This room also boasts of a magnificent fireplace. Two bronze caryatids by Delaplanche, allegorical expressions of Comedy and Dance, frame the marble mantelpiece ornamented with bronze garlands and shield. In front of the richly-framed mirror overhead is a curious urn-

Aiglon salon : detail of the arches, medallion portrait of the composer Boieldieu.
On the overmantel, marble high-relief, "The Abduction of Proserpine". All these architectural features are listed.

shaped clock. Its circular face has Roman numerals and revolves on a horizontal axis, while the urn is supported on fine bronze figures of Neptune and Minerva, the whole flanked by flambeaux.

The décor in the *salon de l'Aiglon*, beside the *salon impérial*, is no less splendid in conception and execution. It too is unusually large at 165 square metres. For the oval central panel and the four rounded panels in the arches Faustin-Besson chose allegorical scenes celebrating marriage. The corner bas-relief portraits are of Boieldieu, Auber, Adam and Lulli. The sculpture

work in this room equals that in the *salon impérial*. Over the monumental fireplace in dull marble there is a quite remarkable high relief white marble representation of the abduction of Proserpine.

Some original features of any hotel are bound to disappear as renovations are carried out from time to time. One such at the *Inter-Continental* is the winter garden which was extremely popular and greatly admired, particularly for its Moorish room, regarded as one of "the most wonderfully oriental spots in Paris".

The gourmet restaurant La Terrasse Fleurie and its summer garden, under the arcades of the main courtyard.

Newspapers of the time spoke of "a fragment of the Alhambra transported by the wave of a magic wand, where arcades and mirrors tirelessly repeat the motifs of the décor, where Oriental divans are shaded by palm-trees".

It is not possible to tell the whole story of the hotel since it first opened its doors. However, space must be found for some of the more outstanding events. In July 1880 the members of the Franco-American Union for the Statue of Liberty held a historic meeting from which a manifesto

issued with the sculptor Bartholdi among the signatories. On the 25th of February 1883, two years before his death, Victor Hugo presided at a banquet given in his honour. In 1887, the management installed an ultra-modern "dynamo-electric" machine which fed the 500 incandescent Edison lamps lighting the public rooms. In the 1900s, two gilded bronze candelabra of unusual size and workmanship were placed on either side of the rue Castiglione entrance to the hotel. They came from a palace in Saint Petersburg. During the First World War, the President

Evening at the Terrasse Fleurie.

The terrace of the Moorish salon in the 1900s. It stood where the restaurant is now.

of the Council, André Tardieu, and the President of the Republic, Gaston Doumergue, had various auxiliary services set up in the hotel. In the Second World War, the Ministry of Foreign Affairs moved into the *Inter-Continental*, during which time one of its best-known officials, Jean Giraudoux, worked there.

Among the celebrities who stayed at the hotel during the *Belle Epoque*, mention must be made of the Grand Duchess Charlotte of Luxembourg, the singer Adelina Patti, the explorer Savorgnon de Brazza, Queen Marie of Roumania, King Peter of Serbia, King Fouad of Egypt. After the Second World War came Marshal Juin (he lived there between 1946 and 1948), Lyndon Johnson (before he became President), John Lindsay, Mayor of New York, Senator MacCarthy, the writer Philippe Erlanger (a permanent resident from 1945 to 1969), and many others.

In 1968, modernization work began on the 500 bedrooms, and new lounges were added. There were proposals to build an underground parking lot and to create a terrace restaurant on the top floor, but these plans came to nothing. After remaining for many years the property of the Achille-Fould family, the *Inter-Continental* passed to a Dutch group, then to Pan-Am, now gone out of business. The establishment belongs at present to the Japanese group Seibu-Saison, and the manager is Frank Mielert.

THE LANCASTER

Atmosphere

Unexpectedness is part of modern travel. Such unexpectedness as confronts the traveller who arrives for the first time at 7 rue de Berri, drawn there by the legendary reputation of this haven only a stone's throw from the bustle of the Champs Elysées. Could the taxi-driver have made a mistake ? Could this really be the place where so many of the famous have chosen to stay : Rita Hayworth, Noel Coward, Clark Gable, Marlene Dietrich, Alec Guinness, John Huston, Gregory Peck, Michael Barychnikov, Peter Sellers, Dirk Bogarde, Ella Fitzgerald, Harold Pinter ? Behind this simple façade ?

Yes, indeed. Like Marie-Antoinette, they all came here seeking refuge. Marie-Antoinette had the whole of Versailles at her disposal. But the palace and its splendours eventually counted little to her, much less than her modest Hameau. The queen preferred the Hameau with its disguised treasures, its quietness, its intimacy. Today many of the rich and famous prefer to stay, not at the *Ritz* or the *George V* or the *Plaza*, but at the *Lancaster*. They are attracted by this snug retreat, which from the outside looks more like the residence of a successful professional man than a hotel.

The Lancaster's discreet charm is not for everyone, and it's not a matter of cost. To appreciate it demands a certain fineness of response. To be able to savour the blue of a July sky, on the patio, having lunched beside sweet smelling honeysuckle and delicately-coloured fuschia. To enjoy the satin feel of a piano in one of the suites, or the porcelain in the bathrooms. To delight in discovering Old

Preceding pages, left :
corner of the Marlene
Dietrich suite, with clock
and portrait of the great
actress. Right : Minerva
dominates the patio.
Opposite : fan frescos and
Von Steinberg's portrait of
Marlene Dietrich.
Right : the dining-room
with its set of 18th
century East India
Company porcelain and
another collector's piece.

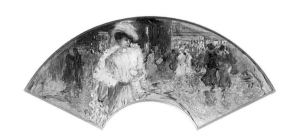

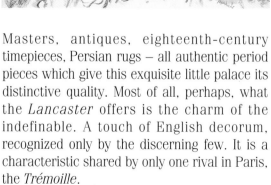

Masters, antiques, eighteenth-century timepieces, Persian rugs – all authentic period pieces which give this exquisite little palace its distinctive quality. Most of all, perhaps, what the *Lancaster* offers is the charm of the indefinable. A touch of English decorum, recognized only by the discerning few. It is a characteristic shared by only one rival in Paris, the *Trémoille*.

Although the visitor is in the heart of Paris within earshot of the Champs Elysées – sunk in a deep armchair, admiring the soft-toned frescos, sipping the finest pink champagne – he is also in the world of the Savoy chain of hotels. Small select sitting-rooms, flower-decked foyers, a riot of works of art, guests conversing in appropriately low tones, service which anticipates wishes – these things reveal the Savoy touch, which prompted one English writer to say that one has merely to touch a bell to command immediate service. The Savoy group – owner in London of one of the most exclusive hotels in the world, the famous

There is a story about *Claridge's* that a caller requesting to be put through to the king was likely to be asked : "Which one ?" This is not mere anecdote. The royal touch is part of the history of great English hotels. The *Savoy* is king of them all, a noble monument to the art of the hotelier. Indeed there is an actual royal connection, for the Queen of England, in her capacity as heir to the Duchy of Lancaster, owns part of the site. It was at the *Savoy* that the celebrated French chef Escoffier created *Pêche Melba* in honour of the great Australian soprano. It was at the *Savoy* that George Gershwin composed "Rhapsody in Blue".

The story of how the *Lancaster* – this jewel of a hotel, this patch of Old England on French soil – came into being is simply told. In 1879, the Prince and Princess of Hennin sold a plot of ground to a certain Santiago Drake del Castillo. Ten years later del Castillo built himself a four-storey residence there, which his descendants sold in 1925 to a Swiss hotelier, Emile Wolf. With a sure instinct, the latter converted the building into a hotel which still looked like a private residence. When he added four more storeys, he kept to the principle of completely separate apartments. Moreover, wisely leaving in their original places the works of art acquired with the building, he used his profits to enlarge the collection.

Thus, in mid-century, there appeared on the patio – where a hundred years earlier horses were stabled – a Minerva and two fauns in bronze by Pompon, accepted in settlement of a countess's unpaid account. Many of the objects that make the hotel a little museum today were acquired during the Wolf era. It is under-

Connaught, and also of *Claridge's*, of the *Berkeley* at Piccadilly, of the *Savoy* itself – does not believe that standardization has any place in the art of the hotelier. They hold that a great hotel needs an understanding of luxury, communicated through the style of the manager, the assiduity of the service, the tactfulness at the reception desk. Many English hoteliers, masters of their profession, learned all this at the Savoy school, as well as the most difficult lesson of all – how to attract crowned heads.

Most of the Regency-style suites have a fireplace.

standable that the management does not like to talk of the matter. A collection of this quality, apart from the respect it inspires in Sotheby's and Christie's, might well arouse undesirable attention. Fortunately, the treasures are well guarded : Louis Seize desks ; bronze animal figures by Barye, scores of rococo consoles ; an unattributed painting of The Battle of Fontenoy ; canvasses by Ziem, Pastoukoff, Cocteau ; an eighteenth-century procelain dinner-service once owned by the East India Company ; rosewood Regency chests of drawers ; marquetry ; marbles ; candelabra ; crystal chandeliers ; silk hangings ; a Persian carpet in every bedroom, every bedroom different from any other, except that in all of them there is a fire-place.

The *Lancaster* can boast of having almost as many staff as bedrooms. Sixty rooms, of which seven are suites, ninety-six beds. You need have no hesitation in putting out your shoes to be cleaned ; in the small hours they will be soundlessly removed and returned, beautifully polished. The service is quite exquisitely courteous, with a courtesy unruffled by the most bizarre requests. Nothing is too much trouble : as a matter of course your shopping is done, your appointments made.

Graceful attention to detail comes naturally at the *Lancaster*. The American journalist, Joseph Wechsberg, reports : "If Madame is lunching alone while her husband is at a business meeting, she will not be placed at a

table in the middle of the dining-room but in a secluded corner, and nobody will suggest that she sign a bill". The same writer records that the *Lancaster* spends more on flowers than on electricity.

Emile Wolf thought his establishment sufficiently quiet, discreet, expensive to attract those for whom cost was no object and for whom comfort was everything. No swimming-pools ; no glass-cases with handbags and perfumes ; no sunroom or fitness club ; no newspaper kiosk. He preferred another kind of distinctiveness. The Laura Ashley sheets, for instance. The English photographer, Richard Avedon, having spent a night at the *Lancaster*, declared that he would never sleep in any other sheets and asked the hotel to supply similar bed-linen for his New York apartment. That sums up the specialness of the place, where French elegance blends with English taste.

Wolf called his hotel the *Lancaster* to attract a clientele who liked things English. In the twenties titled Englishmen and Englishwomen thought nothing of crossing to Paris for the weekend. He got permission from the city of Lancaster to adopt its name and coat of arms. This lordly hotelier retired in 1970. "I have no clients", he used to say, "I have only friends." No group other than the Savoy could, in his view, carry on the tradition of his noble house.

A fair number of those listed in "Who's Who" have stayed, and still stay, at rue de Berri. Among the first was King Umberto of Italy ; another was the extraordinary Nizam of Hyderabad. Well-born visitors genuinely loved the place. Before long, the *Lancaster* was all the rage among stars of stage and screen, especially those from America. For a time, it was like a Parisian antechamber for Hollywood. It could tell many a story about all those folk : Ava Gardner, Marlene Dietrich (the Blue Angel has left her name on one of the suites), Tennessee Williams, Silvana Mangano, Rex Harrison, the Burtons (sometimes known as the Taylors), Billy Wilder, Kim Novak. Joseph Kennedy came too, as did John Steinbeck, Robert Capa, Orson Welles.

The English Queen Mother lunched there one day on the famous patio, almost unrecognized.

Three of the Lancaster's legendary guests : Clark Gable, Rita Hayworth and Marlene Dietrich.

*Opposite :
another suite showing
the "Savoy touch".
Below : view of the patio,
a pleasant place to enjoy
an excellent meal in
good weather.*

The story is still told of how one of the staff took the Duchess of Westminster to be her own lady-in-waiting. The exuberant Duchess of Bedford was not in danger of a similar misadventure. Nowadays at the *Lancaster* you will find the kind of businessmen who do not believe in sacrificing everything to the pursuit of profit. The hotel offers a genuine refreshment of mind and body after a day in the city. Not so long ago, the management suggested that instead of making telephone calls direct, guests might give the switchboard staff the pleasure of being charming to them

while making their connection. For many a guest the head telephonist, Mme Baumier, is a trusted friend. She, in a sense, is the guardian angel of the place. She has seen it all...

She remembers throngs of American film stars, directors, producers arriving with their cabin-trunks for six months filming in France. She remembers John Huston disembarking from the boat-train with secretaries, assistants and chauffeurs, to stay at the hotel during the making of "Moulin Rouge". Over the years, she has seen Ava Gardner arrive with three different husbands, the last of them Frank Sinatra. Three husbands, too, for Elizabeth Taylor. Those stars who filled the place with film talk were Mme Baumier's friends. Evenings at the *Lancaster* were brilliant with the glitter of the American cinema, followed later by the Italians, who took over to some extent. Still, some continued to arrive from America, like Paulette Goddard, Darryl Zanuck, Jennifer Jones, Audrey Hepburn, Mel Ferrer, Gene Kelly, Dino De Laurentiis.

Then there were the musicians, Bruno Walter, for instance, or Richter. And the politicians. Today Milos Forman, Rupert Everett, Pedro Almodovar have their turn in the limelight, if such a word can be allowed in speaking of a place which has never sought publicity. The shade of M.Wolf still presides and the present management has the gift of keeping tradition alive in little details, such as making sure that a client is always addressed by name. Small wonder if the ghosts of those who saw the opening day in 1927 still linger there.

Take your time, you ghosts from the past. The eighteenth-century clock by the door won't insist on the time. Look about you – nothing has changed. Only Alfred, your famous Alfred, is missing. Or is he ? There is a sense in which Alfred – head-porter for forty years – is still on duty. In any case, he deserves a page in the history of the *Lancaster*, counsellor and social secretary as he was to two generations of guests. It was Alfred who looked after the children, sent medicaments all over Europe, found missing husbands, wives, offspring. On one occasion, he filled a huge thermos flask with a cassoulet and took it to Orly for dispatch to Rome, where Elizabeth Taylor was longing

for a taste of that Toulouse speciality. When Curd Jurgens, who was staying at the *Lancaster*, fell in love with Simone Bicheron, staying at the *Trémoille*, it was Alfred who delivered a hundred roses to the lady every morning . After a seige of fifteen days and fifteen hundred roses, Mme Bicheron capitulated and became Madame Jurgens N° 4.

Alfred, that honoured member of the Golden Keys, the International Association of Head Porters, clearly would deserve not a page, but a whole chapter to himself.

LA TRÉMOILLE

"*Fair as a star*"

The Golden Triangle has a gem at its heart, hidden at a point equidistant from the avenue Montaigne, the avenue George-V and the Champs Elysées. A little alertness will discover it, a small hotel of the first order – one might almost call it an inn, with its half-Parisian, half-English atmosphere. This most secret place has a charm that is old-fashioned without being in the least antiquated. You sink into a warm seclusion. In winter a wood-fire, delicately oak-scented, crackles on the hearth.

Your first impression might be that, instead of entering a luxury hotel, you had wandered into a private club, of the kind favoured by experienced travellers who like something out of the ordinary. You are struck by how easy and relaxed everybody is, guests and staff. Steinbeck, the American novelist, once wrote that to

arrive in Paris is to feel immediately taken to its heart by this city which is so much more than a city. That is how you feel as soon as you enter *La Trémoille*. You are immediately among friends, you are part of the family. It doesn't feel like a hotel. It is simply Paris.

What is the source of the name, which does not resound in the history books, but which American and Japanese visitors to Paris find in their guide-books ? Who or what was La Trémoille ? Louis, Lord of La Trémoille, was in fact one of the great names of the Renaissance. This *chevalier sans reproche* (like the hotel) was born during the reign of Louis XI of France, on the 20th day of September 1460 at the château de la Trémoille at Thouars, in Poitou. (The name is pronounced Trémouille.) He began his military career when Charles VIII gave him command of an army of twelve thousand men

Preceding pages : left, one might well be in a charming English home. Right : in the entrance hall, double portrait from the Renaissance period. Opposite : Philippe Noiret, actor and gentleman, was a permanent resident. Below : one of the bedrooms, with its period furniture and quiet comfort.

with which to discourage the overweening ambitions of the Dukes of Brittany, Orléans, and Orange. The Italian wars gave La Trémoille further scope for his remarkable military talents. He fought at Venice, afterwards at Dijon, where he sent across to the enemy lines the most potent of all ambassadors – a convoy of waggons loaded with the wine of Burgundy. Negotiations were concluded in a state of general euphoria, thanks to La Trémoille's shrewdness and his excellent wine.

In 1515, at Marignan, La Trémoille was again in command. After this battle, in which the commander's son had been killed, the French and the Swiss made the "perpetual peace" which precluded for ever any renewal of hostilities between them. After pacifying Normandy, La Trémoille died in 1525, shot through the heart during the battle of Pavia. He is buried at Thouars in the church of Notre Dame beside his son Charles and Gabrielle de Bourbon.

One of the salons before renovation.
Below : detail of a 17th century Aubusson tapestry on the main staircase.

The passage of time has given a curious posthumous fame to the lord of la Trémoille, as to the count of Crillon, whose names would otherwise be lost in oblivion. For each of these long-dead warriors has given his name to a hotel, where he stands, portrayed in painting or equestrian statue, to welcome those in search of the good life.

La *Trémoille* was built in 1863, and has several times been completely renovated and refurbished. Today, it is an oasis of calm, comfort and intimacy in a quarter famous for high fashion and expensive jewellery. The nearby *Plaza-Athenée* and *George-V* do not in the least overshadow it. All three are part of the same chain of hotels, and they serve complementary functions. Clients of the two larger places may choose to dine at the Trémoille, or even to move to it for the sake of seclusion, with everything going on the same bill. Anyhow, for such sumptuous quiet in a busy quarter, who would count the cost ?

nerous size are required. In *La Trémoille*, even the so-called "little" bedrooms are large, and each has its individual, personalized décor. The pride of the establishment is the king-sized suites and the fourteen "junior" ones.

All this is well worth a visit, short or long. Orson Welles was so susceptible to the hotel's charms that it became his favourite resort, where the aroma of his cigar seems still to linger. Doubtless, at the *Trémoille* more than anywhere else, the creator of "Citizen Kane" felt himself a citizen of Paris by adoption. It is the same story with other famous clients, celebrities from the world of the arts, of the theatre, of *haute couture*, people who prefer tranquillity and a hint of romance to what a bigger hotel has to offer. The guests here are more restrained ; the décor is more subdued. It is a soothing place, with its well-chosen pictures that invite inspection and its impeccable service at the touch of a bell.

Main entrance hall today. Orson Welles felt at home at La Trémoille. He loved luxury hotels, and always returned to this one.

Wood, rich hangings, deep, inviting armchairs, Louis Quinze furniture, nineteenth-century paintings, fresh flowers on the tables — these are the features of the décor. Each of the hundred and twelve bedrooms is a model of modern comfort and convenience. To combine elegance with such amenities as air-conditioning, cable television and private safes, rooms of ge-

If you should open a door by mistake, and find what is everywhere a possibility nowadays – screens and charts and busy people in the middle of a seminar, that only goes to show that *La Trémoille* is thoroughly aware of the modern world. But you are much more likely to find an elderly English gentlewoman for whom time stands still, sitting quietly by herself before a Directoire fireplace. The *Louis d'Or* restaurant, more properly styled a dining-room, with orchids on the tables, is ideal for an elegant private dinner. The food is for connaisseurs : traditional French dishes with subtle touches of *nouvelle cuisine*. Sometimes at peak hours there may be a faint hum of talk from media people at the bar, never loud enough to disturb the privacy of the dining-room. Even the chance "golden boy" with his pretty girl-friend would not dare to raise his voice here.

The only snag in this idyllic house is that you are tempted to yield unreservedly to its spell. The enchantment it works verges on the dangerous. When you emerge on to the pavement and the Rolls isn't waiting for you – and there are fewer and fewer Rolls – or the taxi doesn't turn up immediately, you find it difficult to readjust to the exigencies of the real world. You are tempted to go back to be cosseted again by the superlative service within.

Lovers of this kind of hotel are fortunately in no danger of disappearing. What the *Trémoille* offers is not easily found elsewhere. So it continues to attract the discerning. Today, for example, one of its clients is the actor Philippe Noiret, whose elegance and distinction, like the hotel's, is as much English as French. It is the Paris home of this courteous gentleman, so sensitive to proper ceremony and comfort. Philippe Noiret is to *La Trémoille* what la Belle Otéro was to the *Hôtel de Paris* in Monte-Carlo – a sort of presiding genius.

Other actors past and present have loved *La Trémoille*. It is close to many theatres, like the

Théâtre des Champs-Elysées, and to the cinemas where premières are held. Among those who have chosen to stay there rather than at the *Ritz* or the *Crillon* or the *Plaza* are Lee Marvin, Glenn Ford, Tony Curtis, Richard Gere, Jacqueline Bisset, Gene Wilder, Ornella Muti, Michael Reagan, Yehudi Menuhin, Bo Derek. It would be impossible to list all who stay incognito in this hotel which is, paradoxically, both small and great.

At the corner of rue de la Trémoille and rue du Boccador, an inconspicuous façade hides secret harmonies. Come and savour the exquisite nocturne for yourself. There are a thousand reasons why you should.

THE LOUVRE

Between two royal palaces

It is the privilege of this luxury hotel to be surrounded by historic monuments and palaces : the Opéra ; the Comédie-Française, work of the architect Victor Louis ; in the square opposite, two massive fountains sculpted by Carrier-Belleuse and Mathurin-Moreau in 1874. Another few steps bring you to what was once the palace of the duc de Richelieu, later a royal residence, and now houses the Conseil d'Etat. Opposite the terrace of the *Brasserie*, in what is called "the antique dealers' Louvre" you will find within a short radius more works of art and precious objects for sale than anywhere else in Paris, and on the other side of rue de Rivoli, the Louvre itself, the largest museum in the world, with the Musée des Arts décoratifs beside it.

The *Louvre* hotel was the first of the great Paris hotels, for the *Meurice*, though establi-

shed during the Restoration period, moved into that category only at the end of the 19th century. In 1854, Emile and Isaac Pereire had founded "The rue de Rivoli Hotel and Property Company", which put up the buildings between rue de Rohan and rue du Louvre. The largest of these was purpose-built to be *le Grand Hôtel du Louvre*, and was opened in 1855 on the occasion of a reception given by Napoleon III to industrialists and inventors come to Paris for the first *Exposition universelle*.

The *Hôtel du Louvre* at once became one of the grandest places to stay in the city. In October 1855, the "Charivari" was unstinting in its praise. The following from "La Presse" is an example of what was being said in the papers : "Its opening was a red-letter day in the annals of Paris hotels. It has brought a new dimension to the hotel business, catering

Preceding pages : left, the entrance hall. Medallion shows the hotel by night, seen from one of the fountains in the square in the foreground. The bar at the Louvre hotel, as it was before restoration.

as it does for the throngs of visitors arriving by train and steamboat. The *Hôtel du Louvre* will be the model for all such future establishments. The architect Alfred Armand has made its internal layout a masterpiece of practicality ; by the originality of the design and by its impressive proportions, it has already taken its place among the monuments of Paris. We have been given a palace where the public may sleep, facing that other palace where kings used to sleep".

Contemporaries admired in particular the massive four-door entrance in rue de Rivoli, the great *cour d'honneur* under its graceful vaulted roof, later to be imitated in the *Grand Hotel*, the front steps with their four balustrades, the portico carried by five arcades of Corinthian pillars, and the caryatids of the enormous clock, created by the sculptors Klagmann and Choiselet to symbolize the four corners of the world. In the words of one journalist : "The dining-room is the temple of fine food in Paris. It could easily

Opposite : the bar at the beginning of the century. Below : tables at the Brasserie, under the arcades of Place du Palais-Royal.

accommodate the marriage feast at Cana or Balthazar's feast. Is there a palace in our city which can make such a claim ?"

Before occupying its present site, the *Louvre* stood on the other side of the square, under the same roof as the *Grands magasins du Louvre*.

General Boulanger was undoubtedly the most celebrated guest ever to stay in the hotel. With his wife and daughters, he took up resi-

dence there in 1855, occupying apartment 283. Tributes to the man they called "General Revenge" came pouring in from all sides. (He owed his nickname to the fact that in the eyes of many Frenchmen he alone had the courage and energy needed to erase the humiliation inflicted on France by the Franco-Prussian War and the loss of Alsace and Lorraine.) He left the hotel every morning to go to his office at the Ministry of War in rue Saint-Dominique, having first taken his daily exercise on horseback as far as

the Champs Elysées. "Tunis", the General's famous black stallion, was kept in the hotel's stables.

On the 13th of July 1886, a torchlight procession of two thousand people escorted General Boulanger back to his hotel. On the following day he was given an enthusiastic ovation at Longchamp. On the evening of that same day, the 14th of July, the well-known *chansonnier* Paulus launched his latest song "En revenant de la revue", and by so doing, established Boulanger as a national hero. By 1887 the Minister for War was so irritated by the General's popularity that he moved him out of Paris to a post in Clermont-Ferrand. Writing in "L'Intransigeant", Rochefort used the word "deportation", and urged the people of Paris to demonstrate in protest. On the 8th of July, a densely packed crowd surrounded the *Louvre*. The general left the hotel in an open carriage and was cheered all the way to the gare de Lyon.

Ten years later, Camille Pissarro took an apartment at the *Louvre*. From the windows of that first floor apartment, he painted rue Saint-Honoré, place de la Comédie-Française with its fountains, avenue de l'Opéra with its omnibuses. In January 1898 he wrote to his son Lucien : "I've two good-sized rooms and I can see

avenue de l'Opéra from my windows. It's just the view to inspire a painter. I've already started work on two pictures". A hundred years later the *Louvre* goes on welcoming its esteemed visitors with all due attention.

The hotel now has 190 rooms and 22 suites, some of them, like the one where Pissarro stayed, looking much as they did in the painter's day. A complete overhaul is under way since 1987, supervised by the interior decorator Sybille de Margerie. The foyer, the reception area, the bar and the brasserie have already been completed and the banquet hall, the small salons and the bedrooms are in the process of redecoration. The brasserie, with seating for 130, is in deliberately plain neo-Directoire style: black granite floor, mahogany bar-counter, light-coloured wall-covering. A wide bay with *trompe-l'oeil* decoration reveals the arcades of the Palais-Royal. On the walls are four aerial photographs of the hotel. In the main reception lounge, which can accommodate up to 200 people, audiovisual equipment is available for seminars and ceremonial dinners. The glass roof which once lit this neo-Classical room has been preserved intact and may be put back in place in the course of future renovations.

THE LUTÉTIA

A luxury liner in port

More than two thousand years ago, a fleet of little boats came up the river now called the Seine. They were carrying Celtic seamen and fishermen, who built a settlement on the island which is today L'Ile de la Cité.

In 52 B.C. the Romans arrived at the same place, and founded on the south bank of the river a town which they called *Lutetia Parisiorum*, thus immortalizing the name of those Celtic adventurers. Lutetia gradually expanded on that same left bank, destined to be the birthplace of so many adventures.

This is where a luxury ship lies at anchor in Paris today, on the left bank of the river, in a city owing its origins to Celts and Romans. The *Lutétia* of the twentieth century, recalling by its name past centuries, looks forward with confidence to the century to come.

Jean d'Ormesson of the Académie française has defined a luxury hotel as a place of dreams for folk who have come from abroad. The builders of the first Paris did indeed come from abroad. But is the *Lutétia* confined within that definition. Is it merely such a place as M. d'Ormesson imagines ? is it not also something more ? We shall see if answers emerge as we go on. For the moment, let us just say that it is proud to be the only hotel in its class on the Left Bank.

With its glorious history equal to that of any of its rivals across the river, with its illustrious guests and its page-boys in their old-world red livery, this establishment of high repute may be described as in its natural element in Paris, where it stands at the junction of the rue de Babylone and the rue de Sèvres. Some observers find the structure curiously over-elaborate, but the *Lutétia* makes no apologies, sure in the knowledge that for count-

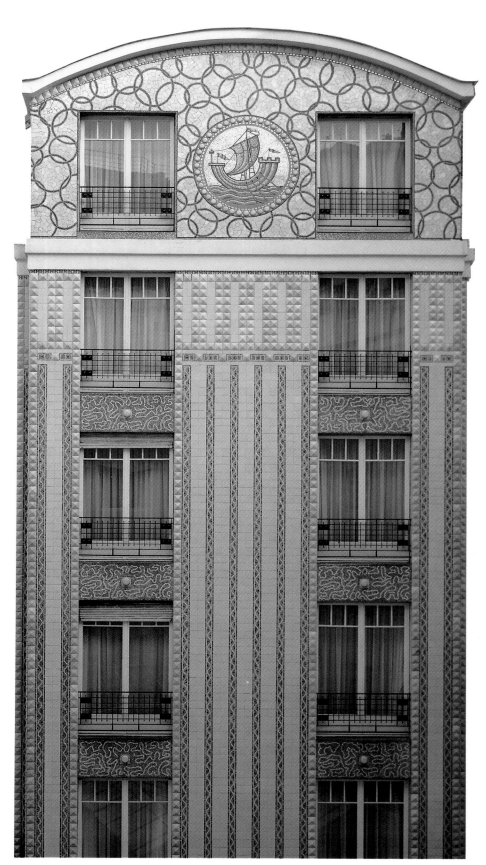

less visitors it is in the first rank of hotels. Like a good ship, it has kept a steady course through the twentieth century – some would say steering backwards ! How is this ?

In 1910 the motorcar and the luxury hotel were suddenly all the craze in France, the two crazes going together for people with money to spend. Paris was an exciting place to be, with the great couturiers launching the new fashion for frills and flounces. La Belle Epoque had arrived, with its taste for the overstated, the over-decorated. Visitors poured in. The *Grand Hôtel* and the *Meurice* were there to receive the rich and famous, and M. Ritz was establishing himself as a formidable rival to M.Levasseur. Now, what about building another rival on the other side of the Seine, where there was no luxury hotel at all, and using a motif of grape-vines on the façade, in memory of the vineyards that had flourished there when the city was still Lutetia ? Once launched, the idea took off, and three years later, in 1910, the *Lutétia* – what other name was possible ? – opened its doors.

The architects were Henri Tauzin and Louis Boileau (who had designed Au *bon marché*, the great department store). Léon Binet and Paul Belmondo (father of the well-known actor), created the façade with its garlands and bunches of grapes symbolic of the abundance within. The original façade, still in excellent repair, has been embellished by wrought iron balconies where the theme of full and plenty is restated in the patterns of vines. It's a shame that so few people lift their eyes to admire all this workmanship – do have a look at it the next time you pass that way.

And what of the choice of position ? A visitors' guide of the time, singing the praises of Paris, has this to say: "The *Lutétia* stands in one of the most salubrious parts of Paris, opposite square Bon Marché, where daylight streams in through the ample windows of its well-ventilated rooms. Visitors will admire the elegance and grace of the building. It is close to various forms of public transport : several omnibus routes, and stations of the *Métropolitain* and the *Nord-Sud* lines". The Métro was then barely ten years old.

Entering the hotel today, we find ourselves in a carefully preserved *Art Deco* world, so well maintained that it looks set to live for ever. The spirit of the original interior design has been conti-

nued in everything added over the years, so that we see on all sides Lalique chandeliers, gold and grey glass along the staircase, opalescent panels set in wood panelling of geometric design, period furniture which ephasizes the deliberately old-world atmosphere. It is a worthy monument in this city rich in fine art, a proper point of departure for a tour of Saint-Germain-des-Prés, where eight centuries of history are enshrined in churches, chapels, museums and in the great town houses of the French aristocracy. When it is lit up at night, the *Lutétia* stands above all these like a beacon.

Although it opened in 1910, the building was not completed until 1912 with the addition of the annexe which was part of Boileau's original plan. On the subject of the façade, here is what Henri Tauzin wrote in the journal "L'Architecte" : "The statuary brings to the ensemble an element of French *joie-de-vivre*, drawing its inspiration from one of the glories of our country, that vine which clambers over every point of purchase to reach the pinnacle of its highest gables". Which just goes to

Preceding pages : Sonia Rykiel's Art Deco design for the Paris restaurant (left) recalls the pleasure of transatlantic crossings. Also shown, the famous grape clusters and cherubs on the façade.

Opposite page : detail of the architecture designed by Boileau and Tauzin.

*Left : Sonia Rykiel and André Gide.
Below : the original awning over the main door.*

Entrance hall in the 1950s, with bell-boys in the livery of the time.

show that literary aspiration was already rife in that part of Paris !

Between the wars, the American bar at the *Lutétia* was a Mecca for all those seeking to discover the real Paris and its literature. Budding talents were toasted there every day, and Parisians loved to come there to have a drink in the company of the "travellers", as tourists were called at the time. If you so chose, you could continue your discussion in the deep armchairs of the Conversation Room, or retreat to the Correspondence Room to write home. The most elegant balls and afternoon receptions at the *Lutétia* found particular favour with women guests, and were held in a setting evocative of literature and the arts with motifs of golden vineyard harvests. This décor was created by Jaulnes, a Swiss artist in vogue at the time. His work may also be seen at the *Bristol*. Were held at the Lutétia, where the interior décor picked up the motif of golden vineyard harvests in the paintings of the Swiss artist Jaulnes, whose work may also be seen in the *Bristol*. Sometimes a guest would venture across the river to the *Ritz* to enquire for Hemingway, always faithful to the hotels on the Right Bank.

Those hectic, bohemian years brought fame to many cafés on the Left Bank – the *Dôme*, the *Rotonde*, the *Coupole* – because of the celebrities

Above : Entrance hall today. Modernization has not changed the atmosphere. Clients are still welcomed with a ready smile.
Below : the Lutétia's famous façade. The hotel is a prominent landmark at the Sèvres-Babylone junction.

who chose them as their stamping-ground. There you could see Derain, Picasso, Vlaminck, Cocteau, Radiguet, Breton, Milhaud, Honneger, Poulenc. The district might be called the golden triangle, with the *Lutétia* at the very heart of it, rejoicing in its high international reputation. In the dining-room, substantial traditional fare was served à *prix fixe*, and after dinner the smoke-filled billiard-rooms were crowded with Parisians and visitors alike until the small hours of the morning.

Like two or three others in its class, this hotel saw French political and cultural history in the making. Many eminent French men and women preferred it to the *George V* with its foreign film-stars.

The first really renowned reservation was a room booked for one night by a twenty-nine-year-old French officer, on leave from duty on the Polish border, who arrived with his bride Yvonne Vendroux. The honeymoon night must have left happy memories, for Charles de Gaulle came back to the *Lutétia* whenever he was in Paris. A former head porter recalls de Gaulle's hurried departure when war was declared in 1939, and the request he sent to the hotel at the time of the Liberation. He had left a travelling bag in 1939, and he now wanted to have it collected. Which shows that nothing goes astray at the *Lutétia* ! History also relates that the hotel was one of the main centres of the Resistance in Paris, and that after the Liberation it took in the

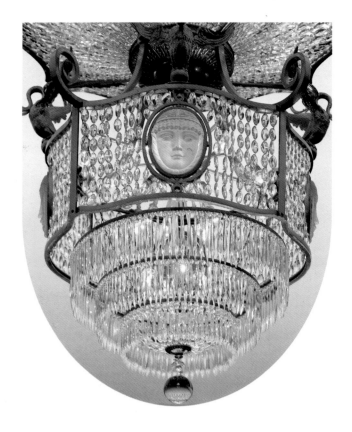

first prisoners returning from the concentration camps. Pierre Gascard's novel "Paris, un jour d'avril", gives a graphic account of the part the *Lutétia* played in the Resistance.

In the post-war period, the centre of political and artistic café society shifted from Montparnasse to such new establishments as Le *Flore*, *Lipp*, Les *Deux Magots*. Yet the *Lutétia* held its position as middle ground between Montparnasse and Saint-Germain. While Juliette Gréco was delighting jazz fans in crowded cellars, the nights were still brilliant at the corner of boulevard Raspail. Electricity – still a luxury at the time – illuminated champagne parties beneath the grape-vines. Josephine Baker was one of the many celebrities to stay regulary at the hotel, where she introduced her children to her friends in a suite lit by the new-fangled bulbs.

"See everything, hear everything, say nothing" is the motto of the ideal head porter. And it is certainly difficult to conceive of any member of the Association of Golden Keys breaking that unwritten law which prohibits him from publishing his memoirs. All self-respecting hotels have their secrets, and keep them – although one or two have been revealed for this book ! Which doesn't, of course, prevent legends from circulating. Did this or that

happen in such or such a hotel ? Was it at the *Lutétia* or the *Inter-Continental* ? Take the story of the prince who desired to send a thousand roses to the lady of his dreams in Cairo. No problem. The head porter bought the flowers, hired a container and personally delivered the monster bouquet with a card bearing the single word "Paris". That anecdote, perhaps apocryphal, symbolizes the proud boast of the Golden Keys that nothing is impossible in the service of a client.

Monsieur Jean, head porter at the *Lutétia*, never lets the visitors' book out of his sight. He was good enough to tell us the story of a former president of a journalists' union who had bought a new hat and thought the brim was too wide. The head porter of the time, whose motto was "No need to ask, it's already seen to", was required to solve the problem on the spot. So he put the hat down on a lavatory pan and trimmed it by following the curve of the bowl. The owner was delighted with the result.

It is quite true that the head porter is confidential private secretary to many guests in a hotel. Some of them just say to him as they arrive "It'll be the usual". A good Golden Keys has a comprehensive address book, containing every name that he could possibly be called upon to supply. He

Preceding pages and above : subtle harmony of colours in bedrooms and suites redecorated by Sonia Rykiel and Sybille de Margerie. Smaller suites on the top floor have a charming salmon-pink décor.

Opposite page, above : print showing ballroom scenes at the Lutétia in the 1920s. *Below :* main reception room today, with rich red velvet décor.

is a mine of information on travel agencies, airline companies, theatres, consulates, where to buy whatever a client may have in mind. A head porter has been known to be guarantor to the management for a client who had lost his credit cards. But don't go too far – there are limits. There can be no question of finding professional female company for a client, since the prosecution some years ago of the management of one hotel – not the *Lutétia* – for providing just such a service.

Yet a head porter will always take the client's side in a difficult situation. On one such occasion at the *Lutétia*, the exuberant Coluche, true to his provocative principles, emptied jars of yoghurt from his bedroom window on to the heads of the policemen who had come about his car illegally parked ouside the hotel. In spite of their best efforts, the police failed to discover the culprit, even though every porter in the place knew perfectly well who was responsible. The following day, the "Figaro" thought fit to warn any of its readers who might be walking past the *Lutétia* to cross the road at that point.

The *Lutétia* is one of the very few great hotels that still accepts guests as permanent residents. Matisse and André Gide used to live there, as Pierre Bergé and the sculptor César do today. They

both have suites furnished and fitted to their own taste and personal ideas of comfort. César considers himself so much part of the establishment that he took a hand in the redecoration of the hotel. So, even if you don't see the artist himself when you visit the *Lutétia* bar, at least you'll see some of his work. And while you're there, you may as well sample the fare in *Le Paris*, the hotel's starred restaurant, or look in on literary luminaries who meet at its celebrated *brasserie* to chat and admire themselves in the mirrors by Slavik.

In the early eighties, the *Lutétia* entered a new phase when it was taken over by the Concorde group (owners of the *Crillon*, the *Hôtel du Louvre*, and the *Concorde-Saint-Lazare*). Sixty million francs went towards restoring the latest acquisition to the position of prestige it had managed to retain during the war and the German occupation, only to go into decline in the postwar years.

The commission to redecorate the hotel went to Sonia Rykiel and Sybille de Margerie. They chose a style which might be described as a blend of *Art Déco* and *Art Nouveau* in which they achieved the most up-to-the-minute comfort without any loss of old-world atmosphere. They aimed at recreating the original décor in the suites and bedrooms

with beautifully restored period pieces : marquetry dressing-tables and wardrobes, octagonal bed-testers. A carpet with geometric motifs was specially designed to emphasize the thirties look. On some floors, the colour-scheme is grey and pearl, or rich red and gold. On the sixth and seventh floors, where the most extensive renovations took place, the colours are delicate salmon pink or floral shades. Up there you find today's regular guests, such as Marcello Mastroianni, Catherine Deneuve, Maurice Druon, Pierre Sallinger, Françoise Sagan, Bernard-Henri Lévy and Hervé Bazin, the last of whom has been a constant visitor at the hotel for the past twenty years.

Still on the topic of comfort, television has been admitted, a bowing to the inevitable, no doubt, but in the form of state-of-the-art equipment receiving up to twenty channels. As a counterbalance, perhaps, the bathrooms are in the most traditional black and white.

The salons are a veritable metaphor for the art of good living, a genuine treat for anyone who appreciates beautiful things. It's absolutely essential to linger, to open your eyes and really take in what you see. No one of these twelve rooms is like any of the others. The *Saint-Germain* has a lovely window from the mid-twenties, and the smaller *Borghèse* and *Conseil* have a special intimacy. The most prestigious of the salons is the *Président*, with marble pillars, wonderful crystal chandeliers and a fully equipped stage, where plays are regularly performed and which lends itself to the many other ceremonial occasions which take place all through the year. The *Lutétia* is one of the few hotels which enter fully into the cultural life of Paris. It presents jazz concerts and operas as well as theatrical performances and exhibitions. Seminars and conferences are daily occurrences, with all the usual technology laid on.

It must be said that the charm of the setting contributes greatly to the success of all these events. The *Lutétia* believes in the influence of flowers, of spots of glowing red, of warmly rich panelling, of tempting armchairs, of natural or softly filtered lighting, of thick carpets. It likes to produce the paradoxical effect of being welcomed into one's own home. "We don't think of ourselves as a luxury hotel", explains M.Jean-Marc de Margerie, the general manager. We flatter ourselves that we are a hotel with atmosphere. "And in that he is perfectly correct."

In this idyllic haven with its three hundred soundproofed bedrooms, seventeen of which are suites, there is a distinctively Parisian gaiety, perhaps not unconnected with the fact that a quarter of the clientele is French, a record proportion. Of course, not everybody who visits the *Lutétia* is necessarily occupying a room. The great liner receives on board many part-time sailors, like the *Amis du Lutétia* who come together on Tuesday evenings for a drink and a chat.

Is there anything more to be said ? Paris is a beautiful city to visit even briefly, and the name of the *Lutétia* keeps its spirit alive by reminding us of its long past stretching back to those first Celtic settlers. The Romans gave it a name, but ancient Rome was far from imagining what is in store today for those who pass through the doors bearing that name.

THE MEURICE

Abode of kings

Great hotels are costly places. You can't but wonder if the game is worth the candle – or rather the candelabra. There is always the danger of being so dazzled by the grandeur that you overlook the details which account for much of the cost.

In our journey through the great hotels, each with its characteristic features, we enter now the uniquely rarefied atmosphere of the *Meurice*, which inspires a respect verging on awe. If today the glory of this veritable palace may seem somewhat dimmed, the hotel can well afford to give that impression. In a sense, varying modes of glory have always been part of its style : sometimes making the headlines, it is always royal; sometimes eventful, it is always luxuriant. In any mode, it has always maintained a world-wide reputation for excellence.

Only the *Grand Hôtel* is as exclusive as the *Meurice* – twin stars in the galaxy of great French hotels. Since 1817 the *Meurice* has played a significant role in the saga of Paris life and French culture. Like the *Ritz*, it is a myth. Indeed, according to some documents, it surpassed the *Ritz* between 1920 and 1940. Given its sobriety today, it is not easy to imagine what this hotel once was. It appears at present to be setting out in another direction, entering a new phase.

Grand brush strokes are needed to evoke the rich past of the *Meurice*, such as one might use in recreating the colourful history of the part of Paris where it stands – around the rue de Rivoli and the Tuileries – where so many epoch-making events took place. We have already told the story of the *Crillon*, bound up as it is with the story of the Place de la Concorde. The story of the *Meurice*, a stone's throw away, is linked to the history of the Louvre, and to that of the former Palais des Tuileries, built during the Renaissance by Catherine de Medici, with its gardens designed by Le Nôtre on Colbert's instructions to replace the village where glazed tiles were manufactured in the 14th century.

Let us move forward now to the destruction during the Revolution of the *Feuillants* – the religious house where the remnants of Louis XVI's supporters made their last stand. In 1810, the first *Meurice* was established on the site, just beyond rue de Castiglione and rue du Mont-Thabor, between the cloisters of the monastery and the famous *manège des Tuileries* where the king's trial had taken place.

Augustin Meurice, born in Pas-de Calais in 1738, had been involved in the stage-coach building in the north of France. Being an enterprising man, he realized that the business of carrying travellers could be developed profitably by lodging them as well. In 1771 he established an inn bearing his name at Calais, where it can still be seen today. When the fall of Napoleon brought English visitors back to France after the long absence due to the Revolution and the Napoleonic wars, the staging-post at Calais became the key junction for traffic between France and England. And every day the Calais coach deposited travellers in rue Saint-Honoré, near the place where the monastery had stood, after a journey of a mere thirty-six hours!

And so, M.Meurice opened his inn in Paris, designed to attract upper-class English visitors for whom silver cutlery would be a "must". The *Meurice* quietly established a distinctive style and came to be known all during the nineteenth century as an excellent place to stay. In London, it was recommended to intending travellers. According to an early brochure discovered by Pascal Boissel :"The bed-linen is washed with soap, not beaten or scrubbed as is the common practice in France" and "There are special rates for persons travelling alone and for families ; for full board, wine included, by the day or the month. Meals may be taken at the *table d'hôte* or in a private apartment. No further expense is incurred other than that of firewood, which the traveller may purchase should he so desire". A mark of the hotel's repute among English visitors is that

an English aristocrat insisted on being brought there to die after being fatally wounded in a duel in the bois de Boulogne.

This was the period when Baron Haussmann launched his massive project for rebuilding Paris. In the Saint-Honoré district alone, forty streets and five hundred houses were swept away. In 1835 the *Meurice* was relocated on a prime site along the newly created rue de Rivoli, where its façade ran the length of forty of the street's arcades.

During the July Monarchy and the Second Empire, this new version of the *Meurice* emerged as a luxury hotel, although private bathrooms were not installed until 1890. From then on the *Meurice* – "the hotel opposite the Tuileries", as it always advertised itself – outdid most of its rivals in the saga of the great hotels of the world. The highly trained staff spoke fluent English. King Edward VII could not conceive of staying anywhere else, making one condition - that meals should not last more than forty minutes while he was in residence. The elaborate dinners might last from eight o'clock in the evening until the same hour the following morning, with on the menu all sorts of exotic dishes such as the swan's eggs mentioned by one traveller.

The third and present version of the *Meurice* dates from 1907. The new owner, Arthur Millon – former waiter turned major-domo turned entrepreneur – wanted to compete with the newly-opened *Ritz*, no less. He embarked on major renovations where everything was planned to the last detail, including hygiene, which was not always a consideration at the time. A management report of the period draws attention to the liftable carpets, the system of copper pipes running up through the building from a suction-pump on the ground floor, and the relentless banishment of all bed-curtains. Millon appointed as manager a remarkable Swiss hotelier, Frédéric Schwenter, to whom the *Meurice* owes its world-wide reputation. From childhood, Schwenter had wanted to become the hotelier of kings. After cultivating his extraordinary flair in Germany, Austria, Italy and England, he was appointed at the age of twenty-seven as manager of the *Savoy* in London. He was later manager at the *Prince de Galles* in Paris (see the relevant chapter), and at other comparable establish-

Preceding pages : a Rolls
arriving at the Meurice in
the 1930s. Also shown,
one of the hotel's many
frescos and paintings.

Left : the splendid
restaurant, as it was and
as it is today. Since June
1990, the restaurant
occupies its original
commanding position on
the ground floor, near the
Tuileries. A charming
spot, with its mouldings,
marbles, painted ceilings,
mirrored doors.
Below : one of the earliest
drawings of the Meurice.

ments. He was the greatest manager of them all, a kind of genius, a supremo in his profession.

With the prize-winning architect, Henri Nénot, Schwenter first reconstructed part of the hotel. Between them, these two men turned the *Meurice* into a royal palace, applying the most innovative architectural ideas. In their scheme, high ceilings were no longer confined to the first-floor drawing-rooms ; they made the great salon on the ground floor, the present *salon Pompadour*, soar into space. The purchase of the neighbouring *Métropole* enlarged the *Meurice* as far as rue de Castiglione. The all-over cost was eight million francs of the money of the time, money well spent, as shareholders would soon discover.

The "Figaro" of the 13th of April 1907 contained the following : "There are rumours at last of the re-opening of the *Meurice* which for several months has been in the hands of workmen and craftsmen. If we are to credit those who have contrived to obtain a glimpse of the renovations, an astonishing transformation has been achieved. Only the façade and, the unique situation of the old hotel have been retained. The rest, it would appear, is the epitome of magnificence, comfort, luxury on a scale never seen before".

Everything was indeed successfully ordained in accordance with the Schwenter philosophy. Madame Swenter herself saw that no speck of dust was allowed to settle. Her husband may not have been as flamboyant as was M. Ritz, but he insisted that the Liège lace curtains in the *salle des Courriers* be freshly laundered and starched every day. It wasn't easy for his staff to sustain such pressure, both moral and professional. During a long postal strike in 1909, M.Schwenter took measures characteristic of the man: to avoid inconvenience for his clients, he sent their letters by special messenger to London, to be posted from there to their various destinations throughout the world.

When the new interior decoration was finally revealed, the newspapers went wild in their zeal to describe it. The dominant style was Louis Seize, especially in the countless reception rooms on the ground floor, free imitations of the great salons in the château at Versailles. The *salle des Tuileries* had the largest carpet ever

Opposite : one of the original salons. Below : one of the suites as it is today, as welcoming as ever. The Meurice offers a unique style of luxury.

produced at the Aubusson workshops. There was a magnificent reading-room, and a replica of Marie-Antoinette's sedan-chair cleverly engineered as a lift. The lift was used in François Truffaut's film "Mata-Hari", starring the incomparable Jeanne Moreau, and is still on show today on the ground floor, a true museum-piece, with its charming little curtained windows. While it was in service, people queued to enter it, and so be carried aloft to what may be called the crowning glory of the hotel.

For M.Schwenter had created an open-air restaurant, the *Roof-Garden*, with a unique view over Paris and the valley of the Seine, right up to Saint-Germain-en-Laye. This gastronomic Mecca had its own kitchens, and the tables were separated by low walls covered with trellis-work and greenery, where electric lighting sparkled at night. The *Roof-Garden* became a favourite meeting place for fashionable Paris.

While the work of renovation was in progress, the workmen found that a little greyhound bitch had taken up residence on the site. It was adopted by the staff, and became the hotel mascot. It is commemorated today in the hotel's crest, where the original animal has been given a companion, in a design symbolic of the house.

Many writers have mentioned the *Meurice*, in particular Léon-Paul Fargue in his book "Le Piéton de Paris", where he declares : "Kings and Queens all over the world added the *Meurice* to the list of their abodes as soon as word went forth that the hotel had reopened". Fargue reported the touching words of a little girl living nearly who spent hours at the corner of rue de Castiglione whenever she heard that a crowned head had come to the hotel. When asked why she was so persistent, she explained : "I'm waiting to see if those ladies and gentlemen look like their pictures in my stamp collection".

Parisian dandies, foreign noblemen, intellectuals, artists : all wanted to be seen at the *Meurice* ; all had something to show for their visit. Edmond Rostand, author of "Cyrano de Bergerac", became one of its most regular patrons whenever the demands of his life as man of fashion and man of letters drew him from his estate at Cambo. It was in the peace and comfort of the *Meurice* that he finished "Chanteclerc". The

Salvador Dali was one of the legendary figures who stayed at the hotel. He has not been forgotten. The Dali years have left their mark.

117

The Meurice was one of the few hotels with a reading room and card rooms (opposite). Members of the aristocracy often came to tea at the hotel in the hope of encountering royal personages.

dinners he gave at the *Roof-Garden* were often in the news.

One of the most distinguished clients of the newly restored hotel was a young man of twenty with dark velvet eyes, privileged from the moment of his birth to be called Alfonso, king of Spain. The young monarch had his own furniture brought to the hotel from Madrid. When he had to go into exile in April 1931, he turned to the *Meurice* where he was joined by his whole family. He held court there and the newspapers spoke of the "Royalist Spanish Embassy" at the *Meurice*. The Prince of Wales with his brother, the future George VI ; the Bey of Tunis ; the King of Montenegro, expelled from his little kingdom ; an endless procession of royal personages, whether in exile or not, came to the *Meurice*, which could justly claim to be the hotel of kings. They came from the courts of Europe and of the whole world: the kings of Denmark, of Greece, of Italy ; archdukes from Austria ; the Sultan of Zanzibar and the Maharajah of Jaipur.

Frédéric Schwenter remained as manager for more than forty years of unparalleled success. Among his gifts was an unfailing talent for keeping on good terms with the Press. The Paris papers published daily lists of the personalities staying at his hotel or attending one of its many fashionable occasions. The *Meurice* served as a kind of tourist barometer. A columnist in the "Gaulois" wrote : "There is a sure way of reckoning the number of foreigners arriving in the capital. You have only to lunch or dine at the *Meurice*, where fashionable Paris and our most distinguished visitors may be seen every day".

In works of literature as in the newspapers, there are many accounts of the *Meurice* in its hey-day. It is mentioned in some well-known novels, as for example in the Countess de Ségur's "Jean qui grogne et Jean qui rit". Here is a curious document, discovered by Pascal Boissel, who has done so much to keep the legend of the hotel alive. "A speciality of the *Meurice* is to attract eccentrics, at least those of them who can pay to bring their crackpot ideas there. For instance, the Englishman who travels with a compass so that he can always sleep with his head to the north, or the American who simply *must* be able to see the Eiffel Tower from his window. When we asked a colleague where he thought

King Albert would stay, he replied without the slightest hesitation : "At the *Meurice*, of course. That's where kings and princes always stay".

As for their queens and their princesses, they had close at hand the pleasures of shopping in rue de la Paix and place Vendôme. The caricaturist Sem sketched a typical *Meurice* client : a gentleman whose stiff collar is so high that the points have become ear-trumpets. He is of course immensely rich, but his wife doles out his pocket-money for each day.

A random sampling of "Meurician" stories yields these events. In 1932, Coco Chanel held reception after reception, sometimes with Marshal Pétain as guest of honour. In 1935, one great occasion was the banquet celebrating the wedding of Pablo Picasso and Olga Koklova, with Cocteau and Diaghelev as witnesses. Franklin

The actress Arletty often came to Florence Gould's fashionable literary luncheons. Arletty gave a party at the Meurice on her eighty-seventh birthday.

Furnishing and décor
have often been changed
without losing their old-
world charm. The hotel
continues to acquire
valuable pictures and
rare items of furniture at
Sotheby's and Christie's.
Righthand page : the
terrace today, and an old
print of the Roof Garden.
Fashionable Paris flocked
to it in Frédéric
Schwenter's day.

Roosevelt, Anthony Eden, Gabriele D'Annunzio, Ginger Rogers all regularly gave or attended parties at the hotel. There was constant traffic of designer-label trunks in the foyer.

The war years were an interim in the glittering history. On the 14th of June 1940 the *Meurice* was requisitioned by the German authorities and became the staff headquarters of the army of occupation in "Gross Paris", with the code-name "Hypnosis". The hotel continued to function, staffed by such personnel as had not been conscripted – with the exception of the reception-desk and the switchboard, both manned by Germans. The entrance to the cellars, camouflaged by a mountain of baskets, remained undiscovered throughout the occupation.

During the battle for the liberation of Paris in August 1944, Hitler had ordered the destruction of the capital before evacuation. There was heavy fighting around the *Meurice*, but eventually calm was restored and the Allies in their turn used the hotel as a base for various operations, such as the search for pilots shot down during the war. Von Choltitz signed the German surrender in the great salon on the first floor. Then in 1946 the Meurice recovered its civilian status and there began a series of renovations that went on until 1972.

At this period it became fashionable in large private houses in Paris to remove wood panelling and replace it with a more modern décor. Much of what was taken out was soon gracing a number of the great hotels. In this way, the Meurice improved its style once again, entering a new era of art and fashion, installing in the renamed salons various antiques, together with statues and pictures whose originals are in the Louvre.

A dominant figure of that period had an elegant walking-stick, waxed moustaches, a faintly Catalan accent. This was Salvador Dali, after Picasso the most popular painter of the twentieth century. Dali and his wife Gala felt at home in the *Meurice*. For thirty years he spent as least a month there every year. The *suite Royale* became his Paris home. There are endless Dali stories. One day he discovered that the polished wooden lavatory seat had been replaced by a plastic one. "Where", he roared, "is the seat of Alfonso XIII ?" And the hotel was turned upside down to find the object, which later adorned a wall in his villa at Cadequès.

But the Master knew how to win the affection of the staff. His eccentricities were never resented, even when with a few strokes of his brush he turned the walls of his suite into a Paris square ; or when he had a herd of goats brought into the corridors and fired blanks at them. After his visits, the whole floor used to be repainted to obliterate his creations. (Was that such a good idea ?) On one occasion, he scattered gold coins in front of the hotel, so that he could drive over them and boast : "I'm doing a golden lap of honour".

Another remarkable feature of the post-war *Meurice* was the literary salon which Florence Gould, wife of the American multi-millionaire Frank Jay Gould, used to hold for several years in the *suite Royale*. Florence Gould was a French-American born in San Francisco. She had married a railway magnate, had been prominent in the hectic post-war years, had loved much and laughed much. She was a highly cultivated woman, genuinely devoted to art and literature. An encounter with Marcel Jouhandeau gave her the idea of organizing luncheon parties at which artists and intellectuals could meet and talk. She had the wit to bring together at those

Thursday gatherings people of opposing views, and her parties became important occasions where it was often possible to predict who would be the next member of the *Académie Française*. In the suite would be heard the sound of her distinctive voice, the swish of her ropes of pearls, and the click of her powder compact which indicated that the session was at an end.

Paul Léautaud and François Mauriac often helped Mrs Gould to draw up her list of guests and to arrange the seating. Not to be invited to the *Meurice* salon was to be out of things. The Morands, Maurice Genevoix, André Gide, Roger Nimier, Arletty, Marcel Aymé, François Nourissier, Jean d'Ormesson, were all regular guests. An amusing – or irritating – feature was the behaviour of the hostess's pekinese dogs who liked to water the hem of the curtains ! This colourful patronage came to an end in 1976 after the death of the publisher Denoël. For thirty years Florence Gould had been the literary muse of the Meurice, had founded the Max Jacob and the Roger Nimier prizes, had drawn in her wake (perfumed by Patou's "Joy") the masters and the rising stars of literature. In the early fifties, royal visitors still gave their preference to the *Meurice*. Though crowned heads had become rare, there were lesser luminaries to take their places, dukes and duchesses, barons and baronesses, later succeeded by artists, filmstars, and finally by politicians.

Today an occasional writer or intellectual, remembering Florence Gould and her salon, may return like a pilgrim to rue de Rivoli – or rather to rue du Mont-Thabor, where the entrance to the hotel is now situated. Arletty, for instance, came back to celebrate her eighty-seventh birthday. The most striking figures to be seen there today are Placido Domingo and the conductor Seiji Ozawa. But there, as elsewhere, times are changing. Businessmen make up the core of the clientele, accounting for seventy per cent of the guests, with twenty-five per cent of them American or Japanese. Which explains the number of Japanese restaurants springing up in the district.

Occasionally the panache of earlier times returns to the *Meurice*. On Arc-de-Triomphe Sundays, for instance, the Aga Khan – patron as well as owner – invites a host of famous friends. Furthermore, the hotel has for some time been the choice of diplomats and of heads of state on official visits to France. The Quai d'Orsay always lodges foreign dignitaries either there or at the *Crillon*. The Queen of Thailand and the Dalai Lama have been guests at the *Meurice*.

The hotel has been fortunate in its managers, who have always been men of exceptional gifts – Auguste Meurice, Galais, Millon, Schwenter. At present the position is held by a man highly respected wherever he has served. Philippe Roche is preparing to guide into the new century the newly restored Meurice, now affiliated to the Italo-European group CIGA. In work directed by the Roman architect Maurizio Papini, who created the *Danieli* and the *Guitti* in Venise for CIGA, the ground floor has been substantially restructured. The famous Copper Bar of the fifties is no longer there, but the original Four Seasons salon is the setting for meetings and business seminars. All the bedroom corridors have been newly decorated in Italian style *stucco antico*.

With the help of Sotheby's, the hotel has increased its collection of furniture, antiques and paintings. The magnificent central salon, the *Pompadour*, for generations the meeting-place of wealth and talent, is still the heart of the place, beating to the rhythm of the clear notes of the piano reverberating from the mirrors. The restaurant has been restored to its original position on the ground floor, a truly royal room where a regiment of attendants bear in exotic dishes.

The key to all this is good organization, which may be translated into telling figures: a staff of 238 ; 146 suites, 2 kilometers of corridors, 6 salons. Some monthly requirements : 2500 bouquets of flowers, 2 kilos of caviare, 5,800 bars of soap. The touchstone of excellence in any hotel is service and reception. At the *Meurice*, from your first visit on, they know what suits you, how you like your bed to be made, whether your morning lapsang-souchong should be strong or light. Personal requests are immediately attended to with the kind of alacrity by which the hotel first made its name. Your shopping is collected, your sewing is done. If you so desire, your bags are unpacked and packed. M.Schwenter somewhere or other surely beams his approval.

After so long a history, the *Meurice* is again in the forefront, proudly looking towards a new era

The famous Pompadour salon, where restful piano music may be enjoyed in the afternoon.

of success, an era symbolized by what has been achieved at the Grand Louvre just beside it. If you are fortunate enough to have occasion to survey that symbol of the future of Paris from a balcony overlooking the Tuileries gardens, give a thought there to the *Feuillants*, to Mrs Gould's luncheon parties, to Salvador Dali riding a bicycle around the *suite Royale*, to Madame Schwenter's anxieties, and recall what Alphonse Daudet observed. He was the only one to point out that kings, by nature not easily impressed, were always sooner or later charmed, surprised, conquered by the *Meurice*. That is surely its greatness : the ability to captivate kings.

In "Rois en exil", when the Queen moved down "the long balcony, its fifteen windows draped in pink, which runs along the most beautiful spot in the rue de Rivoli, she was enchanted".

THE PLAZA-ATHÉNÉE

Temple of music and fashion

Avenue Montaigne might be called avenue des Parfumeurs or avenue de la Haute Couture, for, from the Rond-Point des Champs-Elysées to Place de l'Alma, a line of luxury boutiques bears names to conjure with : Vuitton, Dupont, Scherer, Chanel, Nina Ricci, Caron, Dior, Christian Lacroix, Guy Laroche, Cartier, Inès de la Fressange, Marina B., Bulgari, Valentino, Buccellati, and so on. With avenue George-V and rue François Ier, avenue Montaigne is one of the most exclusive streets in this exclusive district, and it is here that the noble pile of the *Plaza-Athénée* has stood since 1911.

Before the arrival of the current purveyors of luxury, the street was already one of the most elegant in Paris. The names of those who made it so are inscribed in bronze on the pavement - Paul Poiret, Madeleine Vionnet, Jeanne Lanvin,

Jean Patou. In earlier times the street was known as avenue des Soupirs. In the 18th century it became avenue des Veuves, apparently because it was the haunt of "widows" in search of happy encounters.

During the Consulate, Mme Tallien had a country house there. It was called "La Chaumière", and was situated where the Théâtre des Champs-Elysées now stands. Between 1830 and 1880, crowds thronged to the famous pleasure-gardens – the *bal Mabille* – which were located close to the site of the hotel.

The *Plaza-Athénée* started as the *Grand Hôtel de l'Athénée*. It was the creation of the banker Louis Raphaël Bischoffsheim, and was then situated in rue Scribe near the Opéra. At that time the hotel contained the theatre to which it owes its name. Ferdinand Bischoff-

sheim, Louis Raphaël's son, sold the establishment in the early years of the century when the great hotels began to go up in avenue des Champs-Elysées. The new owner was Emile Armbruster, director of the Plaza group. He decided to relocate the hotel in avenue Montaigne and had the architect Jules Lefevre build a new luxury hotel there which he named the *Plaza-Athénée*.

From its opening, the *Plaza-Athénée* attracted a cosmopolitan clientele. During the First World War the top brass of the international scene used it as a meeting-place. Mata Hari was a regular guest ; she liked Room 120 overlooking the inner garden. But it was at the *Elysée-Palace* that she was arrested, and it was the *Meurice* that was chosen for the scene of her arrest in the film about her. Jeanne Moreau played the rôle of the beautiful spy.

Between the wars, the influx of cosmipolitan celebrities continued, in particular from North

Preceding pages : left, the entrance hall of the hotel, recently redecorated. In medallion, allegory of Diana the Huntress, an 18th century painting in the restaurant Le Régence.

Above : Mata Hari had an apartment at the Plaza 1916-1917. Opposite : Le Régence, together with the Relais Plaza, is the home of gourmet food in avenue Montaigne. In 1984, 25,000 sheets of gold leaf were used to redecorate the walls and ceiling.

and South America. From the United States came top people like Edsel Ford, John D. Rockefeller II, George Vanderbilt, Mrs Joseph Pulitzer, Rudolf Valentino, Charles Lindbergh. From the world of the arts they came too: Jean Cocteau, Maurice Chevalier, Christian Berard, Paul Colin the poster-artist, Josephine Baker when she was playing in the "Revue nègre" at the nearby Music-Hall des Champs-Elysées. Later came other celebrities such as Jeanine Charat, the marquis de Cuevas, Charles Munch, André Clutyens, Igor Stravinsky, Arturo Toscanini and many others.

The stream of famous guests started again after the Second World War: Stavros Niarcos, Yuri Gagarin, the Kennedys, King Hussein of Jordan, Anthony Quinn, Peter Ustinov, Liz Taylor, Richard Burton, Daryl Zanuck, Ava Gardner, Yehudi Menuhin, Herbert von Karajan, Karl

Yuri Gagarin stayed at the Plaza during his official visit to Paris. The window-blinds strike an exotic note. The patio and its creeper-covered walls, one of the most fascinating places in Paris. The restaurant Le Régence puts out its tables there as soon as the weather allows.

A poster by Paul Colin for the Théâtre des Champs Elysées. The great stage star Josephine Baker lived at the Plaza-Athénée. Below: study-sittingroom in one of the spacious Louis XV suites, with its flower arrangement, renewed daily.

Munzinger, Nathan Milstein, Ornella Muti, Marcello Mastroianni, Woody Allen, Leonard Bernstein, Giorgio Armani. Famous names continue to be common-place at the hotel.

The *Relais Plaza* restaurant, designed by François Dupré in 1936, is part of the hotel, with its own separate entrance. It too has always attracted the patronage of celebrities. Their predilection for the place is understandable. The plate-glass windows shield clients from the stares of passers-by. Inside, Jacques Dupuis's décor is both stately and relaxed : tall mirrors create an impression of spaciousness; flower and plant arrangements add an agreeable touch of gaiety ; a huge bas-relief by Francine Saqui depicting Diana the Huntress dominates the bar. Today Werner Küchler is in charge of this lively restaurant.

The *Plaza* has other attractions besides the *Relais*. The most impressive of all is the exotic *galerie des Gobelins*. This is a spectacular gallery, unusually long and strikingly handsome in design. Pairs of tall Ionic pillars run the whole length of each side of the passage. From the intricate stone-work on the capitals of the pillars soar graceful curved arches whose finely worked ribs and keystones draw the eye upward to admire the wonderful craftsmanship.

All this grace and elegance is dazzlingly illuminated by bronze and crystal chandeliers and wall lights. The gallery is a favourite place with guests, particularly at tea-time or when it is the setting for a fashion-show.

There are several salons in neo-Classical style, all with beautiful panelling, paintings and tapestries – the *Marie-Antoinette*, the *Colbert*, the *Concorde*, for example. The *salon Montaigne* has oak panelling à la *capucine*. In the alcoves opposite the immense bay windows are works by 17th and 18th century French painters.

There is also a gourmet restaurant, le *Régence*, which can seat seventy-five guests. It was established over fifty years ago and completely renovated in 1984. The walls are done in alternating wood and silk panels with tall cornices above ; there is fine plaster-work in the mouldings and medaillions on the ceiling and every where lavish use of gold-leaf. (Twenty-five thou-

Charles Lindbergh, John and Jackie Kennedy, are among the many famous Americans who have stayed at the Plaza.

sand leaves were used in the course of redecoration.) The whole décor glitters in the light of chandeliers and wall-lamps. A handsome Regency-style fireplace gives the restaurant its name. The tables are spread with Porthault napery, laid with Christofle silver and Haviland porcelain from Limoges. In the kitchens a staff of seventy works under the direction of the chef Gérard Sallé to maintain the high reputation of the *Régence* ; five wine-waiters are responsible for presenting fine vintages from the excellent cellar and laying in new stock.

From spring to the end of the summer season the restaurant, which has a staff of thirty-five, spills out its tables under red parasols on to the marble paving of the large inner courtyard. To eat out-of-doors at the *Plaza* is an enchanting experience : the Virginia creeper climbing high on the walls, the red window-blinds, the cheerful sound of the two fountains make it a magical place.

The same fineness of taste is evident in the bedrooms and suites – Regency-style furniture pleasantly consorting with Louis Quinze and Louis Seize pieces ; opulent silk curtains in subtle hues. A characteristic note at the *Plaza-Athénée* is the flower-arrangements ; these absorb a higher proportion of the hotel budget than does electricity.

As Michel Blazy, the present manager of the *Ambassador* puts it : "In the fifties and sixties, the *Plaza-Athénée* was a bench-mark for anyone who wanted to set up a luxury hotel". The tradition of excellence has been maintained by first-class managers, head-porters, head-waiters, head wine-waiters. Among them must be mentioned Georges Marin, a legendary figure in the world of hotels, who was manager from 1951 to 1969, and also his successor Paul Bougeneaux.

The latter had an unusual career. He was head-porter and shop-steward at the *Plaza* when the new owners, Trusthouse Forte, offered him the post of manager. (The Forte group, to which the *Plaza-Athénée* belongs together with the *George-V* and the *Trémoille*, owns nearly eight hundred and fifty hotels all over the world.) Bougeneaux accepted the challenge, and took the bold step of involving the staff in the management of the hotel, so that they shared responsibi-

131

lity for the commercial success of the enterprise. As a result of his initiative, the uncertain financial position of the hotel was set right. Bougeneaux died in 1991, just after becoming chief executive at the *Trianon-Palace* in Versailles. The present man in charge is Franco Cozzo. He first entered hotel business at the *Plaza* in 1962, and was appointed manager in 1979.

The hotel has two hundred rooms and apartments and a staff of four hundred. Service is of a very high quality. Many of the staff have been there for twenty years or more and have detailed knowledge of the individual habits and needs of the clientele.

Paris — Rue Scribe — Hôtel de l'Athénée.

In 1990, the American journal "International
Investor" published a survey of the seventy-five
best hotels in the world. The *Plaza-Athénée* was
ranked sixth.

THE PRINCE OF WALES

Regal elegance

The most famous Prince of Wales today is of course Prince Charles. The title, which dates from the fourteenth century, is always held by the heir apparent to the British throne. The hotel took its name, not from Princess Diana's husband, but from his grandfather, George V, whose coat-of-arms – three ostrich feathers surmounting a crown with the device "Ich dien" (I serve) – may be seen above the entrance in avenue George-V. Each window in the building sports a red awning, which gives an air of gaiety to the neo-Classical façade with its cornices and balustrades masking balconies and loggias.

The hotel is situated close to the Champs Elysées, the Lido and *Fouquet's* and since its opening in 1928 has attracted an international clientele. Before the war, famous visitors included Sir Winston Churchill, Neville Chamberlain,

King Alexander of Yugoslavia, the writer Erich-Maria Remarque, Marlene Dietrich. After the Liberation, actors, musicians and other public figures continued to grace it with their presence : Charles Laughton, Lana Turner, Max Ophüls, Gina Lollobrigida, Dizzie Gillespie, Art Blakey, Nat King Cole, Baron Thyssen, Prince Otto von Hapsburg, Henry Kissinger. More recent clients include the producer Elie Chouraqui, who always stays at the hotel when he is filming in France, and various tennis stars in Paris for the Roland Garros tournament. So what attracts so many well-known personalities to the *Prince of Wales* ?

To start with, there is the quality of the interior decoration. The *Le Panache* salon and the patio-garden with its mosaic floor alone are worthy of being listed as historic monuments. The marble walls of the salon and the gleaming

cut-glass light-fittings are handsome examples
of Art Deco, sober yet elegant in style. In the
thirties, this was a style more popular for ocean
liners than for Parisian hotels.

The blue, yellow and gold motifs of the patio
turn up again in the quite marvellous
bathrooms of the hotel. Such bathrooms –
spacious, comfortable, sumptuously appointed
– are a symbol of the pure luxury which makes
establishments like this so different from
ordinary tourist hotels.

The period bathrooms of the *Prince of Wales*,
so characteristic of the place, are certainly one
of its charms. It's a great pity that the current

*The dining-room with
mosaic floor, pale marble
pillars, wall-lights and
glass roof is an
interesting example of
Art Deco. Today it is the
Prince of Wales gourmet
restaurant.*

management, in the interests of ease of maintenance, plans to get rid of them.In 1985 the hotel was acquired by the American Mariott group which owns 450 hotels and 1,400 restaurants all over the world. It then underwent major renovations. The interior decoration is the work of Robert Lush, who was also responsible for the renovation of the *Café de la Paix* and the *Carlton* in Cannes. In 1992 the *Prince of Wales* was acquired by the Sheraton group.

Today the establishment is managed by Douwe Cramer; the chef is Pierre-Dominique Cecillon. The restaurant is a dazzling place. The Christofle silver and the Bernardeau porcelain on the tables, the paintings and prints on the walls, the superb woodwork, the plants and flowers everywhere make it a friendly and welcoming setting. In summer one can eat out of doors in the *Patio*, the restaurant in the inner courtyard.

Like its peers, the *Prince of Wales* has a highly-skilled and attentive staff. Gaby Willem, for instance, who for forty years has served in the *Regency* bar, and Marc Berthout, the head porter who for twenty years has ensured that the place runs on oiled wheels.

The proximity of the Champs Elysées is certainly a major factor in the continuing popularity of the hotel. But the quality which really brings clients back again and again and which makes them recommend it to their friends as a most agreeable place to stay is the warmth and excellence of the welcome.

THE RAPHAEL

Whisper it only

Your first impression is of gleaming, honey-coloured wood, with here and there rich colours of stained glass. The huge Turner dominating the foyer gives a sense of entering a museum of choice exhibits. Floating rather than walking on the deep carpets, you know that this is a very special place. Here in avenue Kléber you are entering no mere hotel, however luxurious ; you are about to visit a true work of art.

This kind of unflawed elegance seeks no publicity. The *Raphaël* is discreet ; it shuns any showy display ; it is effortlessly at the top of its class. Its guests, many of them celebrities, are men and women of discrimination, forming a club where membership is not lightly bestowed.

First and best : there are never any tourists or businessmen rushing about here, and that is more than can be said of some establishments. The *Raphaël* is extremely quiet even when there is not a room to be had.

By some strange magic, you hardly ever see anybody around; you generally feel the place to be empty, as if the usual fuss of hotel life were miraculously excluded. Yes, miraculous is indeed the only word adequately to describe the effect.

And yet, if the sofas and red curtains in the famous English bar could talk, they might speak of artists, writers, media people, public figures of all kinds, coming here to play their part in shaping the history of our times. Think, too, of all those fairy-tale romances in the charming bedrooms looking out on to the Place de l'Etoile. But let us take our time : there is much to see and to tell.

Preceding pages, left :
this fine wood work, seen
here in the former library
complete with fireplace, is
worthy of its setting.
In medallion, self-
portrait by the Italian
painter Raphaël, the
hotel's emblem.

Right : one of the suites,
showing alcoves,
luxurious décor and
handsome wardrobes.

The hotel was built on a spacious scale in a spacious age, so that all its proportions are generous. The over-all impression is that there is plenty of room everywhere. The bedroom-sitting-grooms are more like apartments, furnished with graceful chairs, Récamier sofas, desks with secret drawers and *trompe-l'œil* book-cases. The bathrooms, with their period china-ware and double wash-basins, are large enough to live in. The lift, on the other hand, is quite small, deliberately cosy. The restaurant, efficiently run by a young staff, is known as "the dining-rooms". Proust would have enjoyed coming here, lover of hotels as he was; he used to say that they were the only places where he was left in peace.

So the *Raphaël*, just beside the Arc de Triomphe, is the most nostalgic, the most timeless of all the great hotels in Paris, one of those where you feel immediately welcome. This palace in miniature is one of the priceless treasures of the city, as foreign visitors inviting their friends to meet them there are well aware.

When "Last Tango in Paris" was being made, Marlon Brando stayed at the *Raphaël*, as did others of the cast. Nobody knows how many ce-

144

lebrities have passed beneath its chandeliers, from the film moguls of Hollywood and Beverly Hills to the great names of world politics. In New York, Tokyo, London, Stockholm, Milan, Los Angeles, among the international jet-set, The *Raphaël* is often mentioned as symbolic of the charm of France.

Let history explain how that came about. This lovingly maintained building is part of a story that began at the end of the nineteenth century, in the mind of yet another pioneer in the creation of Grand Hotels. We have already heard of Jammet, Schwenter, Ritz, Wolf. Now Leonard

Tauber appears, opening in rapid succession three high-class hotels : the *Régence* (three hundred rooms), a major event in 1900, followed in 1907, on the site of the palais de Castille, by the world-famous *Majestic*, reckoned at the time to be the finest hotel in Europe. (It was sold to the State in 1937, was later occupied by the Germans, and now houses the International Conference Centre in avenue Kléber.)

Meanwhile, in 1925, Leonard Tauber built another hotel opposite the *Majestic*, in which he hoped to realize his perhaps unattainable vision of absolute luxury, absolute perfection. He cal-

The original bedroom-sittingrooms with canopied bed and tiled bathroom. Unidentified 18th century painting.

and taste, and he supervised personally every detail of the new building. Every suite had a sitting-room, an alcove bedroom (the alcoves are still there). Several had a boudoir as well as the large bathroom and abundant wardrobes. There was period furniture everywhere. Tauber hoped to welcome to the *Raphaël* the *crème de la crème* of those already coming to the *Majestic*, itself regarded as unsurpassed. Which shows how high he was aiming.

This master hotelier took personal charge of the *Raphaël*, making the whole of the sixth floor his home. A privileged guest would occasionally be allowed to visit his drawing-rooms, library, gun-room, chess-room, and the balconies opening on to the Arc de Triomphe. Great armfuls of roses for the hotel arrived every day by Rolls-Royce from his house at Louveciennes. Leonard Tauber has been fortunate in his successors at the *Raphaël*, for unlike many other proud hotels, it has never seen its reputation waver, and it has remained in the family, controlled, managed and financed from French sources, at a time when so many others have been taken over by international companies.

For more than sixty years of quiet celebrity, the *Raphaël* has been a home from home for many well-known figures in the world of politics, literature, music, painting. The list is endless : the Kennedys, the Rothschilds, Fellini, Rossellini, Burt Lancaster, Mick Jagger, Ava Gardner, Ingrid Bergman, Peter O'Toole, Kim Novak, Gloria Swanson, Romy Schneider, Joseph Losey, Jean-Luc Godard, Jean-Pierre Melville, Robert Mitchum, Harold Lloyd, Gina Lollobrigida, Walt Disney – better stop, for fear of over-kill. Just a few more : Bernard-Henri Lévy, Mickey Rourke, Alexis Weissenberg, David Bowie, Paul McCartney, Yannick Noah, Sylvie Guillem. All of them with the same urgent need : people in the public eye must have a little peace and quiet from time to time. At the *Raphaël*, nobody is on show ; nobody is asked questions or subjected to critical comment. It would be unthinkable to find an autograph-hunter in the foyer, as can happen elsewhere.

The avenue Kléber entrance to this home from home of great stars. Portrait of the pianist Horowitz, a regular guest at the Raphaël before the last war. He returned here after his long absence in the United States. Righthand page, above : a mural painting. Below, Marlon Brando, like many Hollywood stars, was fond of the Raphaël. He stayed there during filming of "Last Tango in Paris".

led it the *Raphaël*. It was an entirely new concept at the time – to put beside a hotel with hundreds of rooms another with the number of apartments deliberately limited, but with all of them unusually spacious and magnificently appointed. Leonard Tauber was a man of culture

Still, since this book requires it, we must extract some memories, some stories, some secrets from this hushed establishment, so reminiscent in many ways of a Venetian palazzo.

146

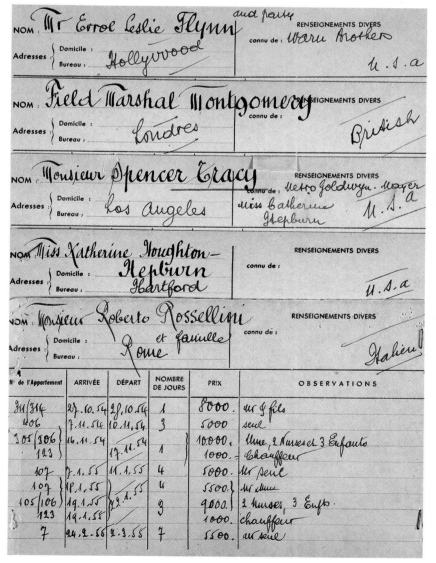

Nobody denies, for instance, that Roberto Rossellini and Ingrid Bergman made their home here in the intervals between films, with chauffeurs, chefs and children's nannies. They were often visited by friends such as Fellini, Carlo Ponti, Sophia Loren. People remember at the *Raphaël* that Rossellini (whose daughter, by the way, comes there today), was allergic to down and silk, and always arrived with his own special pillows. Katherine Hepburn and Spenser Tracy came there as lovers, occupying suite 609, with its romantic view. From the balcony in clear weather they could admire the Eiffel Tower as well as the Arc de Triomphe and the Opéra. Tabloid journalists often pursued the famous couple along avenue Kléber in the early 60s.

The famous English bar at the Raphaël lends a slight air of mystery to all conversations.

The pianist Vladimir Horowitz, who enjoyed the good life, was a faithful client over two periods separated by a long interval. In 1939, the war banished him from the *Raphaël*, and from Europe, where he did not set foot again for more than forty-five years. When in 1986 he did at last return from the United States for a concert performance, he came back to the *Raphaël*, accompanied by his wife, and returned many times after that. On each occasion the management received strict advance instructions on his diet, with a warning not on any account to forget the piano ! Jean-Pierre Melville also will be long remembered at the *Raphaël*, where he liked to do

his work. But in Melville's time, the *Métropolitain* had not yet been modernized, and was still very noisy. The Etoile-Nation line came above ground beside avenue Kléber close by the hotel, shaking the chandeliers in Melville's room, and driving him to distraction by disturbing his train of thought.

For some months before his suicide, Mishima used to come to the *Raphaël* in search of solitude in one of the rooms with a number ending in 7, the best ones according to those who know about such details. There is no end to the strange or exciting moments that are recorded

at the hotel, though space can be found here for only a few examples. In the bar or in one of the reception rooms you might happen upon the ghost of Pasolini, who is supposed to have written some of his "Ecrits corsaires" there. Films have been made there too, some sequences, for instance, of "Grand Bleu", "The Heir", "Un homme amoureux" and "Twist again in Moscow". The staff still talk of Serge Gainsbourg's difficult sessions in the bar, and of one Italian producer who used to send to a bistro across the road for his expresso coffee, because it was more to his taste than the superior sort served in the hotel. Then there was the well-heeled

client who used to send a bellboy to the smart shops to buy Madame's underwear. And they wonder if Mrs Thatcher remembers coming in one evening from a summit meeting and having to take the service lift because the main lift was under seige.

The great German writer Ernst Jünger, who lived for some time at the hotel, has added a foot-note to history by revealing a hitherto unknown occurrence at the Raphaël during the war, when, like most hotels in its class, it was requisitioned by the occupying forces. German generals billeted there entered into a conspiracy to overthrow Hitler, and that these officers, the first to turn against their Führer, were known as the "Raphaelites".

Steeped in memories, inviolable in its hushed tranquillity, the *Raphaël* is sure to be a distinguished address for a quiet meeting with the year 2000 or for taking a rest from Paris in the very heart of the city, within a stone's throw of the Arc de Triomphe. But don't expect to find a sauna or a swimming-pool there – it's not that kind of hotel. It has made only one concession to modern ways by providing private rooms to carefully screened corporate bodies for meetings, seminars and luncheons.

Alain Astier, the present manager, is a passionate defender of the Tauber philosophy and traditions. He considers himself bound to honour the Raphaël legend and to preserve its mystique intact. Renovations are unobtrusive, and there is never any question of tampering with the furniture, for the Raphael must stay as it has always been. The brass beds are still there with their alcoves and canopies ; the old-fashioned baths are still in place ; the predominantly Regency style of decoration will not be altered. Raphaël's self-portrait – well, actually it's a copy ; the original is in Florence – will remain at the reception desk.

Just as the actor Mickey Rourke would remain at the *Raphaël* after it had opened its doors to him as he fled from one hotel to another in an attempt to get away from journalists. "It's funny", he said at the time, "you're right in the middle of town, they all know you're in there, and still, there's some magic that keeps the bloody hacks out."

THE RITZ

No richer jewel

The *Ritz* is situated at Nos.15-17 in place Vendôme, one of the handsomest open spaces in Paris, and one of the very best addresses. Designed by Jules Hardouin Mansard in 1685 on the instructions of Louis XIV and his minister Louvois, it is made up of twenty-eight town houses with a façade of great Corinthian pillars. Its two hundred and ten arcades make an elegant setting for the expensive jewellers and the international banks which occupy those houses today. Place Vendôme takes its name from the town house built by César de Vendôme, son of Henri IV and Gabrielle d'Estrées, on the site where the *Ritz* and the Crédit Foncier de France stand today. The splendid houses in place Vendôme were all owned in the 17th and 18th centuries by great aristocratic or haut bourgeois families. Most are now the property of banks or of international corporations.

During the French Revolution, The Grande Chancellerie took over the houses to the left of where the *Ritz* now stands, which premises it still occupies today. In 1699 an equestrian statue of Louis XIV by François Girardon had been erected in the centre of the square. In 1806, after his victory at Austerlitz, Napoleon had the statue removed to make room for a column to be placed there in honour of la Grande Armée.

Its design was inspired by Trajan's column in Rome. It stands 44 metres high and is crowned by a statue of the Emperor. Around the column spirals a bronze *alto-relievo* 220 metres long, on which hundreds of men and horses represent events in the Napoleonic campaigns. This monument was pulled down during the period of the Paris Commune, on the initiative of the painter Courbet, but was replaced in the following year.

Preceding pages : left, detail of décor in Vendôme salon. In medallion, portrait of César Ritz.

For twenty years Marcel Proust was a familiar figure at the Ritz. Sculptured fireplace at the Ritz Club, in the basement of rue Cambon wing. With its panelled décor, the Club is a pleasant place to meet.

The *Ritz* is at the heart of a quarter of Paris where luxury goods and services may be found in abundance : around place Vendôme itself, in rue de la Paix, rue de Castiglione and faubourg Saint-Honoré.

The *Ritz* is in fact two separate buildings. One of these faces on to place Vendôme, where the architect Charles Méwes preserved Mansart's classical façade. The other, built twenty years later, has its frontage in rue Cambon. The two buildings are linked by a passage 110 metres long, where glass-cases display fashion wear, jewellery and other luxury products from all the best houses. Above these there is an admirable collection of Gobelins and Beauvais tapestries.

You enter the hotel under the arcades, where once clients would dismount from their carriages. Here, set into the ground, is the great bronze crest of the *Ritz*. Once through the revolving door, you find yourself in an entrance hall with the reception desk on the right. This hall opens into a gallery with deep blue carpets and tall windows opening on to the summer garden. The great white stone staircase, lined with tapestries, leads to the hotel's most prestigious apartments, all looking on to place Vendôme : the Imperial suite, the Windsor suite, the Chanel, Proust, Hemingway, Chopin suites, and more. Beside the Vendôme bar is a patio where plants and flowers make a charming setting for sculptures such as the 17th century statue of Pomona under its graceful arcade. The grand *salon Vendôme*, one of the most magnificent in the hotel, also looks out on to the patio. The great windows of this salon are hung with rich curtains of warm-coloured Lyons silk and brocade. Nearby, the *salon de Psyché* has a view over another garden. On rue Cambon side, the garden of the restaurant *L'Espadon* with its rockery fountain is a more secret, more secluded place. Once the fine weather sets in, this is a popular place for dinner. The renowned Hemingway bar is nearby. The Ritz Club in the basement has a handsome fireplace and a pleasing panelled décor.

The founder of the hotel, César Ritz, was born in 1850 in the Swiss village of Niederwald. He arrived in Paris at the age of seventeen at the time of the 1867 *Exposition universelle*, and

began his career as wine-waiter at the famous *restaurant Voisin*. In 1872, he took up a post at the *Hôtel Splendid* in place de l'Opéra. He next moved to Vienna for the International Exhibition in that city, and at the Imperial stand he met the Prince of Wales who was to become his most distinguished client and patron. In 1873 he went to the *Grand Hôtel* in Nice, and after that to Locarno. While he was there, according to his biographers, he began to recognize the primary importance of hygiene in the hotel business. He first put his convictions into practice by introducing the strictest standards of cleanliness at the *Victoria* in San Remon. Not everybody took his ideas seriously ; he was to encounter the same scepticism later after installing new sanitary arrangements at the *Ritz*. "If you fear tuberculosis, there is no need to go to a nursing-home in Switzerland. M. Ritz's hotel is fully guaranteed."

In 1877, César Ritz took over the management of one of the most outstanding luxury ho-

tels in Europe, the *Grand Hôtel National* at Lucerne, owned by the Pfyffer family. Some years later, he went to the *Grand Hôtel de Paris* at Monte Carlo, where he brought Auguste Escoffier as *chef de cuisine* – a move marking the beginning of a highly successful collaboration. In 1889, d'Oyly Carte founded the *Savoy* in London, where this new venture quickly declared itself as the most luxurious hotel in the world, and the rendez-vous of all the best people. D'Oyly Carte invited both Escoffier and Ritz to come to work at the *Savoy*. Ritz immediately put work in train to install the most modern lighting – indirect and filtered – and used the gardens to launch the idea of outdoor dining.

It had long been César Ritz's ambition to found his own luxury hotel in Paris. In 1896, he heard that the *Hôtel de Lauzun* in place Vendôme was coming on the market. He was not in a position to finance the purchase himself, so he set up a company in collaboration with various friends

The Imperial suite on the first floor, overlooking Place Vendôme, is the most prestigious in the hotel. Hundreds of celebrities have slept here, from Woody Allen to Elsa Maxwell.

153

and professional contacts. Among the founding members and principal shareholders were Vicount and Lady de Grey, whom Ritz knew as regular guests at the *Savoy*, Calouste Gulbenkian, one of the pioneers of the petroleum industry in the Gulf, the banker Leonard Hirsch, Sigismund and Ludwig Neumann, Baron Jacques de Gunzburg, Arthur Brand from the Banque Lazard and Harry Higgins.

As Madame Ritz wrote in her Memoirs: "The ceremonial opening of the *Ritz* took place on the 1st of June 1898. Among the guests were Boni de Castellane, the comtesse de Pourtalès, Grand Duke Michael of Russia and the whole Rothschild clan". To these may be added Princess Murat, the marquise de Ganay and the comtesse de Chevigné ; the duc de Rohan, the duc de Marny and the duc d'Uzès together with their spouses ; Grand Duke Alexander, Santos-Dumont, the Goulds, the Vanderbilts, Liane de Pougy, la belle Otéro, Emilienne d'Alençon ; the Dukes and Duchesses of Marlborough, Portland and Sutherland ; Lady de Grey, and – of course – Marcel Proust. What more favourable auspices could be hoped for ?

César Ritz chose Charles Méwes as architect, with the commission to transform the interior layout of the old building. Only the cellars were left as they were. Outside, the classified façade in place Vendôme was left untouched, apart from the opening of the arcades to allow guests to emerge from their carriages under cover. Méwes chose all the furniture himself, designing new pieces when he could not find what he had in mind. Every detail down to clocks, bells, telephones was considered in making each bedroom and suite a harmonious whole. This concern for unflawed harmony was evident in the public rooms too, from the colour of the curtains in the salons to the gold-work in the restaurant.

César Ritz was insistent on one point : he must have brass beds. Every room had its bronze pearl-encrusted wall-clock operated by compressed air. Indirect lighting was introduced in the restaurant by the use of table-lamps. Méwes drew much of his inspiration from 18th century models, and the neo-Classical style apparent in the décor of the *Ritz* had a lasting effect on hotel architecture up till the 1920s – one thinks, for example, of the *Trianon Palace*.

"Outside Paris one might easily believe that Ritz was not the name of a man, but of a monument or a famous place, like Obelisk, Eiffel Tower, Vatican, Westminster, even Jerusalem or the Himalayas", wrote Léon-Paul Fargue, that "Piéton de Paris" who so much enjoyed a little rest in one or other of the great hotels as he wandered round the city.

At the *Ritz*, Proust found yet another home from home to add to Cabourg, Venice and Evian. Up until 1922 he would take from time to

The most luxurious suites at the Ritz are in the Vendôme wing, looking out on the square. They include the Imperial suite, and others named after such celebrities as Proust, Chopin, Hemingway, the Duke of Windsor, Chanel.

vourite hotel. "Do you think I could have a peach or an apricot from the *Ritz* ?" On the 18th of November 1922 he sent his favourite taxi-driver, Odilon, to the hotel for a carafe of the chilled beer he used to enjoy so much. When it came, he was too weak to drink it.

Proust was always interested in the profession of hotelier, which he thought to require great understanding of human nature and to offer so many opportunities of deepening that understanding.

"The *Ritz* is a quiet place ; great ladies whose fortune would enable several generations to live comfortably sip their tea there like elegant ghosts (...) And a last word to those who waste their time making a name as a poet : a smart floor manager in a hotel can easily make more than 10,000 francs a month."

Olivier Dabescat, that Napoleon among *maîtres d'hôtel*, is a legend at the *Ritz*. Debascat began in the hotel business at the *Bristol* in London at the age of twelve. Later, while he was working at *Paillard's* on the Champs Elysées (the restaurant that is now *l'Elysée-Le-nôtre*), César Ritz spotted him.

Olivier Dabescat became as well-known as most of those he served at the *Ritz*. George Painter describes him as tall, distinguished, im-

time a room or a suite according to what he could afford. He noticed that the staff were even more attentive to his needs after he had published "A la recherche du temps perdu" and won the *prix Goncourt*. Olivier Dabescat, *maître d'hôtel* at the *Ritz* at that time, is often described as being dictatorial in his dealings with guests. Yet he was extremely attentive to Proust, making sure that his bedroom chimney was drawing properly and that he was protected from the slightest draught of cold air. When he was dying, Proust was still thinking of his fa-

maculately dressed, slightly alarming in his single-minded dedication, with the charisma of a high-priest, the tact of a diplomat, the strategic skill of a general, and the quick-wittedness of a great detective. "I have given you the best table, sir," he would murmur a dozen times in the same evening to one of his favoured clients.

Madame Ritz had this to say of him: "Olivier was bound to become a character who had to be put in a book, and no great lady would fail to include in her memoirs a couple of stories about Olivier of the *Ritz*".

Edouard Bourdet used Olivier in his play "Le Sexe faible", and Aimé, Proust's *maître d'hôtel* at Balbec, is based on him.

"Wondering whether a guest is in a good or a bad mood is not the business of the staff of a well-run hotel. And yet, travellers richer in heart than in luggage do command admiration." So said Olivier Dabescat after forty years at the *Ritz* – from 1899 to 1939.

The hotel had of course its share of eccentric clients. There was a man called Beny Wall whose dinner partner was his Boxer dog wearing a stiff shirt-front and bow tie. There was the marquise Cassali who kept in her room a boa constrictor with a special fondness for rab-

bits. And there was a Mrs MacLean who always arrived with her pet falcon.

Boni de Castellane once invited his aunt, Princess Radziwill, to dinner at the *Ritz*. He gives an amusing account of the evening. "I placed her opposite me, with her back to the windows, to give her a full view of the exotic company in the restaurant. She was mad about the syncopated modern music, and enjoyed herself like a child doing something rather naughty. Here is a sentence from her letter of thanks : "I'm really pleased and grateful that you took me to that inn where I never dined before" "

The *Ritz* launched the fashion for dinner out-of-doors. A journalist wrote some time around 1905 : "On a fine evening the pleasant country feel of the garden is preferable to the splendour of the dining-room. At the *Ritz*, where the birdsong is sweeter than the violins, blackbirds, thrushes and chaffinches give a concert performance for guests sitting under the trees among the flowers".

The quality of the cuisine was always extremely important, not surprising when one remembers that César Ritz called Auguste Escoffier "the greatest chef in the world". When Escoffier left the *Ritz* to return to the *Savoy*, succeeding him was a daunting task for Gimon, former chef at the Russian embassy.

César Ritz recognized that the man in charge of front-of-house staff was no less important than the master in the kitchens. The head-porter had to be a man of many gifts, personal and professional. Holders of the Golden Keys know many languages ; they also know human nature. They can sum up a newcomer at a glance, and give him the kind of information about Paris that will suit his particular interests, all with the greatest possible discretion. It has been rightly said that the head-porter is the living, unfailing memory of a hotel. There was a time when the head-porter worked his way up the ranks ; that was the case with André Deneux who came to the *Ritz* in 1907 and left it only in 1935.

All the wealthiest and best-known personalities of the *Belle Epoque* could be found sooner or later at the *Ritz*. When the Prince of Wales, soon to be Edward VII, heard that César Ritz hoped to open his own hotel in Paris, he announced : "Wherever Ritz leads, we shall follow". He was as good as his word, staying at the *Ritz* whenever he was in Paris, instead of at the *Bristol* (also in place Vendône) as he had been accustomed to do. Lady de Grey, Boni de Castellane, the Shah of Persia, the Maharajah of Karpurthala and the Russian Grand Dukes Paul, Vladimir, Alexis and Michael were among those who helped to give the *Ritz* its distinctive stamp. Whenever the Russian royal personages were in residence there was always a discreet police presence at the hotel because of the danger of an anarchist attempt on their lives.

In those years the *Ritz* used to issue a monthly publication setting out the main events in the life of the hotel. It records a luncheon party given on the 7th of February 1907 by King Edward VII and Queen Alexandra in honour of the marquis and

Ernest Hemingway and Gary Cooper, two famous guests who helped to spread the fame of the Ritz.

The Hemingway bar in rue Cambon, with bronze portrait of the novelist who used the Ritz for scenes in "The Sun Also Rises".

marquise de Breteuil. After the meal the king had a long conversation with the marquis, who was one of those mainly responsible for bringing about the Entente Cordiale.

Liane de Pougy was often at the *Ritz* in the twenties. In "Mes cahiers bleus", memoirs remarkable for their intelligence and generosity of spirit, she writes : "I like the *Ritz*. It's a place where I can still meet dear friends from the past".

Immediately before the First World War the salon wing was added, as was the building fronting on rue Cambon, linked to the original building by a long covered gallery.

From 1914 to 1918, like many similar establishments, the *Ritz* became a medical centre for officers wounded in action. Great ladies came to the hotel on missions of mercy, and were even admitted into the bar, until then an exclusively male domain. Towards the end of the war, Winston Churchill was a regular visitor.

After the war Marie-Louise Ritz continued to run the hotel with the assistance of Henry Ellés as she had done during her husband's lifetime. In 1919 the then Lord Derby reported after a stay at the *Ritz* that "of all the memories brought back from Paris, the most extraordinary was one of M.Proust", the first person the noble lord had ever seen wearing a fur coat at dinner !

The 1920s were the most flourishing of the inter-war years for the *Ritz*, with such prestigious clients as Calouste Gulbenkian, Barbara Hutton and Mrs Vanderbilt. When Andrew Carnegie arrived he was invited to choose any one of the most splendid apartments from the celebrated *suite impériale* down. Since he was short in stature, Carnegie settled for one bedroom with a view on the garden as more in keeping with his tastes and size. "A pleasing example of modesty and humility, qualities for which the clientele at the *Ritz* is not exactly renowned, though it certainly does include some eccentrics", was the comment of one contemporary .

When the Cambon bar opened in 1921, it quickly became popular with many well-known Parisians, especially with writers and journa-

lists. But the bulk of its clients were English or American. When she was at the height of her fame as a singer, Elsa Maxwell was at the centre of memorable evenings there, together with such people as Cole Porter or Serge Diaghilev and his Ballets Russes. When Charlie Chaplin stayed at the *Ritz*, the universally admired star of the silent screen had to come out on his first-floor balcony to acknowledge the plaudits of the crowd filling place Vendôme.

The Wall Street crash and the international crisis that followed put a stop to such festivities. It was then that César Ritz's son, Charles, had to go on a tour of the United States in an effort to find new markets – the first time the *Ritz* had felt the need to publicize itself. It was then too that Scott Fitzgerald and Ernest Hemingway became regular clients of the hotel they would write about in "A Diamond as big as the Ritz" and "The Sun also Rises", respectively.

Apartments were seldom taken by the year. Georges Mandel lived there from 1920 to 1939, and an unnamed lady of fortune made it her home from 1929 to 1985, with an interval during the war. When Gabrielle Chanel moved there in 1934, she was only the third person to take up permanent residence. The hotel was requisitioned in 1940. Mme Chanel returned after the great June exodus to find that her apartment had been stripped bare. She was given a little room

The Vendôme salon, with its splendid Regency-style panelling and curtains, is on the ground floor opposite the summer garden. It can accommodate up to two hundred people.

Georges Lepré, principal wine-waiter at the Ritz, maître d'hôtel at the restaurant L'Espadon.

kept the place going as she had always done. Many people doubted the existence of such a person ; others believed that even if she had once existed she must be long dead. She was often to be seen, a tiny, elegant figure quietly moving round the great building, but those who met her had no idea that this was the great César Ritz's widow." The American journalist Janet Flanner had described her some years earlier. "She entered the restaurant wearing gloves and hat and carrying a parasol, as if she were not in her own house at all. As she passed, gentlemen rose in their places and bowed. Madame bowed to each in return. Waiters jostled less important diners so as to have room to bow more deeply. She responded to these marks of respect like a queen moving among her subjects. Yet you were in no doubt that not a detail had escaped her."

overlooking her premises in rue Cambon. She lived at the *Ritz*, surrounded by her books and her own furniture, until her death in 1971.

In "What became of Anna Bolton ?", Louis Bromfield describes the hotel in the 1940s. "Within the *Ritz*, however, life went on. Mme Ritz

When Claude Auzello returned to the *Ritz* as administrator in 1940, it was requisitioned by the Germans. He set up a Resistance network operating from the hotel under the noses of high-ranking officers, including Field-Marshal Goering.

Hemingway's version of the liberation of the *Ritz* is mostly fantasy, for he got there only the

The bathroom in a renovated apartment, as luxurious as ever. Note the traditional fireplace.

The Health Club in the hotel basement has ultra-modern equipment. Around the pool, trompe-l'oeil paintings from Catherine Neff's studio.

following day. He arrived in an American army jeep, clutching a sub-machine gun and pretty drunk. After a quick visit to the bar, he had a shower and went to bed. However, he has this to say about the end of a busy day : "The *Ritz* was where the action was, the evening was fine, I downed a couple of Martinis at the Cambon bar. Then I had a good dinner under the chest-nut-tree in the little garden opposite the grill-room. After a few brandies I strolled up to my room and got into one of those Ritzy brass beds. Under my head was a zeppelin-sized bolster and four square pillows filled with real down, two for me and two for my lovely lady-friend."

The following decades were times of high living when celebrities from all over the globe consorted with distinguished Parisians from the worlds of the arts, the cinema, high fashion and industry. During the 1960s the Duke and Duchess of Windsor were often among the guests.

By 1952 Charles Ritz with his wife Monique had taken over the running of the hotel from his mother. They continued to run it until 1976. Meantime, the need to modernize had become urgent, and that would require substantial capital outlay. The Fayed brothers acquired the *Ritz* in 1979 for a price of 30 million dollars ; they paid as much more again on restoration.

Mohamed Al Fayed knew the *Ritz* as a child when his parents had a hotel in Cairo. He left Egypt for London after the fall of king Farouk, and became thoroughly anglicized. He also made a great deal of money. In buying the *Ritz*, he was fulfilling a long-standing ambition while at the same time indulging his taste for preserving what has been handed down from the past.

Franck Klein was appointed manager, coming to the *Ritz* after a long career which took him from the *Savoy* and *Claridge's* in London to the *Ritz* in Madrid and the *George-V* in Paris. His

first duty was to supervise the renovations for which Bernard Caucherel was the architect. All the bedrooms and all the lounges were restored, some of the original bedrooms were run together to make modern apartments, the mansard storeys looking on to the courtyard were converted into magnificent suites. One of these is the Chopin suite, named in honour of the composer, who had lived in a house across the place Vendôme where he died in 1849.

Considerable technical difficulties were overcome to install in the basement a health and fitness centre in the form of a huge swimming-pool of 16 x 7 metres surrounded by gymnasia, saunas, squash courts and hairdressing salons, the whole covering an area of more than 1500 square metres.

The *Ritz* now has 187 bedrooms, 35 apartments and 10 prestige suites. The 500-strong staff includes a number of craftsmen, like the goldsmith whose full-time job is just to look after the hotel cutlery.

According to Auguste Escoffier, true happiness depends on good cooking. Following in this tradition, the *Ritz* has never lost its popularity with gourmets. Guy Legay, holder of the cove-

ted award of *"meilleur ouvrier de France"*, is the *chef de cuisine* ; no fewer than four of his team have that same qualification in their special fields. The restaurant, *L'Espadon*, in the charge of Franco Gentileschi, formerly of *Maxim's*, offers a bill of fare which has gained it two stars in the Michelin guide. The *Ritz* is the only Paris hotel in its class to have its own bakery. The bread and confectionery produced there daily bears comparison in variety and quality with the best that money can buy anywhere in the city.

It must also be mentioned that the hotel opened in 1990 the *Ecole de gastronomie française Auguste Escoffier*. This school run by Georgy Usher, an American who adores French cuisine, offers adult courses lasting from one to six weeks in cookery, confectionery, baking, serving at table and expertise in wine.

Mention of wine brings to mind the cellar at the *Ritz*. In his book "Le Ritz, magie d'un palace et de ses vins", Georges Lepré, head wine-waiter at the hotel since 1983, tells a lively, anecdote-studded story of rare vintages. There are in all 130,000 bottles ; 30,000 are kept in place Vendôme, the remaining 100,000 in a depot in rue Lecourbe. Some of the bottles César Ritz laid down in or around 1910 are still there : 1840 cognacs and ports, 1897 clarets. The stock is of course renewed in every great vintage year. A certain number of bottles are held in store for regular clients. All wines and liqueurs are served in a range of Baccarat glasses specially made for the *Ritz*.

In his preface to Georges Lepré's book, Jean d'Ormesson writes : "For many Parisians, Frenchmen and foreigners, you stand for a civilisation to which the world is indebted and which is itself indebted to wine. There is a sense in which you serve that civilisation as does a musician, a painter, a writer (...) You have poured me many a glass of mineral water and not held it against me. You deserve credit, for you know everything that can be known about wine".

Georges Lepré came to Paris from his native Gers to work at the *Grand Véfour*. He spent seventeen years there before going to the *Ritz*. Working at the *Ritz*, according to Lepré, makes you part of a recognized community. When you are a member, your visiting card opens all doors and even an occasional frontier.

"The *Ritz* is a quiet, decent place, a place suitable for the great of this world to rest their weary heads. Yet it also rings with romance." So wrote Léon-Paul Fargue in 1935. It is no less true today.

Early in the 20th century, César Ritz launched the novel idea of evening meals out-of-doors. This is now a tradition at the Ritz, where diners sit in the Vendôme gardens, the summer garden and on the terrace of the restaurant L'Espadon.

Following double page : the Duke of Windsor suite on the first floor, overlooking Place Vendôme, is an excellent example of the kind of splendour that earned the Ritz the title of king of luxury hotels.

THE ROYAL-MONCEAU

A gracious heirloom

Refinement and discretion, intimacy and respect, relaxation and gastronomy, these are the words that spring to mind. Let us look at the reality that inspires them. It's all around you as soon as you enter this delightful hotel.

Have you ever been intrigued by a certain splendid façade along one of the finest streets in Paris ? Among the avenues radiating from the Arc de Triomphe, avenue Hoche, with its handsome rows of plane trees drawing the eye towards the parc Monceau, has a special distinction all its own, an undeniable nobility. Is in itself a visible sign of wealth. Limousines seem to glide like fish in limpid water to the door of the great hotel we are about to enter, across an invisible frontier into a legendary world where things are ordered differently. Even seen from the street, the *Royal-Monceau* is resplendent,

its very chandeliers expressive of its international repute. And when you pass beneath those chandeliers, it is to discover a rich and various life within, where the most up-to-date facilities are provided in a setting which is literally out of this world.

For example, the hotel has an ultra-modern sports and leisure complex, bearing comparison with the best to be found anywhere in Paris. Yet the atmosphere of the hotel is reminiscent of a colourful Italian-style palazzo, where you are caught up into a life you would like to savour in full measure, to enjoy every detail as generationsof faithful clients have done before you. At every turn, you are caught up into a life you would like to savour in full measure in this colourful Italian-style *palazzo*, proud of its generations of faithful clients.

The hotel took its name from the nearby parc Monceau, itself no stranger to the colourful. During the reign of Louis XV, the duc de Chartres, later known as Philippe Egalité, instructed the famous Carmontelle to create a curious Anglo-Chinese garden. Up until the Revolution, the Duke provided glittering festivities of all kinds in the new garden. Cagliostro displayed his talent as a hypnotist there. Later, after the park became the property of the city authorities,the architect Alphand emphasized its English features by introducing artificial ruins, statues, grottos, ponds. By 1880, it was regarded as the finest public garden in Paris.

After being unveiled in 1836, the Arc de Triomphe became the centre from which several important thoroughfares radiated. Rue Sainte-Marie, already in existence, merged with boulevard Monceau to be called avenue de la Reine Hortense, of which name it kept up until 1879. It was renamed avenue Hoche in the early years of the Third Republic, in honour of Lazare Hoche, a well-known figure during the Revolution, best known perhaps for his suppression in the west of France of resistance to the new régime.

At the turn of the century many superb buildings went up in avenue Hoche, which runs close to the Beaujon quarter of the city, fashio-

nable at the time because of an extraordinary amusement park called *Folie Beaujon.* For anyone wealthy enough to think of acquiring property in the area today, it is difficult to divide honours today between avenue Hoche and avenue Foch, both equally remote from the hustle and bustle of the city centre. The latter avenue, of course, cannot boast of a Royal-Monceau ! To redress the balance a little, avenue Foch sometimes prefers to be known as avenue du Bois, borrowing glory from the nearby Bois de Boulogne.

To return for a moment to the beginning of the century : a great many first-class hotels came into existence in the area around L'Etoile and the Arc de Triomphe for one simple reason – the religious congregations were moving out. In the same way as we have already seen at the *Bristol,* where part of the establishment used to be a convent, scores of religious houses whose orders could no longer afford to maintain them in this expensive quarter were sold for one reason or another in the years before the First World War and were replaced by hotels. Many of them came and went, like the *Elysée-Palace,* the *Mercédès,* the *Astoria,* the *Majestic,* the *Claridge,* the *Carlton.* Others are still prospering today, like the *George-V,* the *Prince of Wales* and the *Raphaël,* all described in this book.

The *Royal-Monceau* stands on the site of a retreat house which belonged to the Augustine Sisters of Notre Dame. It was put there by Pierre Vermond, a pioneer in the hotel business whose name is also associated with the *Ruhl* in Nice, the *California* in rue de Berri, the *Miramar* in Biarritz, and the defunct *Carlton*, mentioned above.

Designed by the architect Duhayon, the *Royal-Monceau* opened its doors on the 1st of August 1928, the year before the great Wall Street crash, as yet completely unforeseen. There was a hairdressing salon with forty seats, a bridge-room in the basement, a table-tennis room, a billiard-room opening into the immense bar, and, of course, a tea-room. A brochure printed to mark the opening extols the elegance of the area, the premises and the clientele. Here is a sample : "In avenue Hoche, spacious, airy, untroubled by autobus or tramcar, the *Royal-Monceau* offers quiet, refinement, and the most attractive décor in Paris behind its blue and gold window-blinds".

1928 was a noteworthy year in many ways, a kaleidoscope of colourful events. On July 23rd, Raymond Poincaré became president of the Council of State and Aristide Briand was back at External Affairs. The Assembly approved a bill presented by a certain M. Loucheur, proposing "a building programme of low-cost dwellings with a view to relieving the housing crisis which has grown so serious over the last ten years".

In sport, it was the year of Suzanne Lenglen and of the Four Musketeers of French tennis, Borotra, Brugman, Cochet and Lacoste. France won the Davis Cup and Georges Carpentier became the idol of the boxing fraternity. André Malraux published "Les Conquérants" ; Marcel Pagnol's "Topaze" carried all before it. In the field of interior decoration, the master glassmaker Lalique boldly combined Art Deco with a neo-classical Greek style, and metal began to be used in furniture manufacture from 1928 onward. In architecture, Robert Mallet-Stevens produced designs incorporating geometric forms, a novel idea at the time.

1928 was also the year of the motor-car. The responsible authorities had made great strides in improving road surfaces, many of them in

Left : statue in main foyer.
Opposite : Les Thermes, the finest health and beauty centre in Paris.
Below : one of the luxurious bathrooms.

very poor condition since the war. At the twenty-second Motor Show in Paris, vehicles within the reach of modest means showed signs of taking over the market from luxurious Packards, Hotchkisses and Hispano-Suizas. Mermoz was about to astonish the world with the first air-mail service without a radio link between France and South America. In the world of high fashion, Paul Poiret's star was setting, Coco Chanel's was rising. Women's clothes were simpler: for day wear, skirts rose to knee-length, a fact not unnoticed by gentlemen ensconced in the armchairs of hotels such as the *Royal-Monceau* ! Hairstyles were short and close to the head. After a visit to the hairdresser, a woman might be greeted by the chant : "She's had her hair cut !".

The world of entertainment was full of excitement. Mistinguett and Maurice Chevalier were all the rage, starring in extravagant American-style revues at the *Casino de Paris* or the *Folies-Bergère*. According to the newspapers, the pair first fell in love when they were rolled up in a carpet for an act in which they would be unrolled on the stage. "Our lips did meet, I have to confess", said Momo afterwards. This was also the hey-day of

Le Boeuf sur le toit, there was afternoon dancing in the tea-rooms where the more uninhibited did the black-bottom and the less daring, the java. As for the *Royal-Monceau* – there, of course, they floated on Persian carpets...

The hotel had instant international success. Pascal Boiddel's researches in its records show that the first recorded guest was M.Avenol, secretary of the League of Nations at Geneva. Rich Americans, maharajahs, politicians of all shades of opinion, diplomats, film-stars, wealthy families (or families which appeared so) and other "beautiful people" : they all came with their retinues of servants to the seventh floor, the whole of which was reserved in the early years for the most distinguished guests.

After the temporary lull due to the financial crisis in 1929, business had picked up again by 1932. During the tense social and political events of 1936, the hotel was a kind of haven. Many meetings on matters political and economic took place in its private rooms during the Third Republic. Joseph Kessel discovered it. General Pétain entertained General Pershing there in 1938. In June 1940, early in the dark war years that nearly every great Paris hotel had to live through in much the same conditions, the French and German delegations negotiating an Armistice stayed at the *Royal-Monceau*. Then the hotel was requisitioned and occupied by German officers. It had one stroke of good luck, in that the German officer in charge was in civilian life a hotelier who had done a course at the *Royal-Monceau* two years earlier. It was no doubt largely thanks to him that the hotel suffered no damage while it was occupied.

In 1945 came the victorious Allies. General Eisenhower and Field-Marshal Montgomery both stayed at the *Royal-Monceau* with their respective staffs. Admiral Kirk, commander-in-chief of the American Marines during the war, made a long stay. When he was leaving, he presented to the hotel the star-spangled banner which had flown on his flag-ship. At a summit meeting of Heads of State at Versailles in 1982, this historic flag was solemnly returned to General Alexander Haig by the hotel management.

Like most similar establishments in the period immediately after the war, the *Royal-Monceau* saw its fair share of diplomats and official delegations. Civilians gradually began to outnumber these, though there were still some important political visitors. Hô Chi Minh stayed there for seven weeks in 1947, during the Fontainebleau conference on relations between France and Vietnam. It was also the scene of meetings preliminary to the setting up of a Jewish state in Palestine, to be called the state of Israel. In what is now one of the restaurants and was then the *salon Louis XVI*, the proclamation of the new State was signed on the 14th of May 1948, in the presence of David Ben Gurion and Golda Meir. in the same year Walt Disney arrived in Paris to receive the Legion of Honour, and stayed in avenue Hoche.

Pascal Boissel, that walking data-base of the hotel world, has found accounts in the hotel's archives of the exotic ways of Eastern potentates who had been guests at the *Royal-Monceau*, where they all arrived with mountains of luggage and hordes of attendants. These picturesque visitors created some intriguing problems. The Maharajah of Indore always required forty-seven rooms to accommodate his harem, while the Maharajah of Kapurthala would send down for live ducks. A certain Hindu magnate installed his private chapel where he performed ritual ablutions before meals. Another, a vegetarian, was the despair of the chef trying to ring the changes on eternal vegetable and rice curries. One nabob straight out of the "Arabian Nights" had his army of bodyguards who took their duties very seriously indeed, and imposed rules of conduct on the hotel staff which took no account of democratic principles. When King Farouk of Egypt was a guest for several months after his exile, his way of life was somewhat nearer to ours !

One may wonder if all these luxury hotels with their Cinemascope fronts are caravanserais from an earlier age, or if they are really part of today's world. When the question is put beneath the cut-glass chandeliers of the *Royal-Monceau*, one finds a certain ambiguity in the answer : places like this have bowed to the requirements of modernity on condition that nostalgia is still allowed. Nostalgia for idleness in a world where the work ethic is paramount. Nostalgia for what lasts in a world where fortunes change hands so readily. The nostalgia of the privileged few, perhaps ?

therine Deneuve, David Bowie, Bette Davis, Claudia Cardinale, Sylvester Stallone, Sting, John McEnroe. Charles Aznavour and Lisa Minnelli stayed here when they gave a concert together in Paris. All these have trodden the deep carpets and marble floors of the pink and beige salons. In the *Aquarius* music-bar, they exchange a nod or a smile, all sharing the same predilection for this club of theirs, a club become a workplace for some of them on occasions when a film is being made at the hotel. The occasional film has been made here. And it has always been a favourite with painters, such as Braque, Dufy, Chagall, Picasso, Matisse, even Dali when he chose to be unfaithful to the Meurice. Our political masters continue to come here as well : George Shultz, James Callaghan, Pierre Elliott Trudeau, Helmut Schmidt, Takedo Fukuda, Huang Hua, Valéry Giscard d'Estaing, Raymond Barre, Jacques Chirac among others. The American ministers James Baker and Dick Cheney were often here during the Gulf War.

The two hundred and nineteen bedrooms and suites provide classic comfort, with those little extra touches specific to the house. There are jacuzzis in the bathrooms, and there is round-the-clock room service. Businessmen may discuss their schemes in comfort in the numerous seminar and conference rooms. The hotel is popular with media people, who often hold meetings or press conferences in the *salon Joséphine*. Over the past ten years, substantial renovations have been carried out without any of the gilt being rubbed off. One of the advantages of this Italian-style hotel is that its clients have at their disposal from 7 a.m. to 11 p.m. a full range of health and beauty services such is not available anywhere else. In the *Thermes*, with its name evocative of ancient Roman comfort, you may have a massage, a sauna, a therapeutic bath, a hair-do, a beauty treatment or a manicure ; you may do body-building exercises in the gym, play a game of squash, or swim in the pool. Nothing is forgotten for the health-conscious : you may have a low calorie-meal served at the pool-side after your swim.

Those more interested in gourmet food than in dieting are admirably catered for in the hotel restaurants, the *Jardin* and the *Carpaccio*. The *Carpaccio*, as the name suggests, specializes in Italian food, more specifically in Venetian dishes. The *Jardin* is acknowledged as one of the grea-

In any case, nostalgia is still permitted at the *Royal-Monceau*. The children of the clients of the fifties come here, their visits less prolonged, no doubt, than in their parents' day, but their ways the same. There are a few long-term regulars who have discovered the hotel that suits them perfectly, like the singer Michel Polnareff for whom it appears to be a haven where he finds inspiration and equilibrium. The suite which he rents by the year has its own little secret garden.

One of the fascinations of such a place is seeing a politician or an oil-baron in the lift with a Hollywood star or a captain of industry. The passing show is rich and various. From the world of show-business, over the past thirty years, it has included Elvis Presley, Jean Gabin, Ray Charles, Romy Schneider, Gene Kelly, Ca-

test restaurants in Paris. Under its bubble-shaped glass dome, which is one of the landmarks in the eighth arrondissement, it has a real garden with trees and flowers around the central rotunda which is the restaurant proper, making a charming setting for a leisurely breakfast or midday meal.

The *Royal-Monceau* has given its name to a chain of hotels, which now includes the *Vernet* in Paris, the *Miramar* in Biarritz. The group also owns the *Louison-Bobet* centres for sea-water therapy. Pleasantly situated as it is a little off the beaten track, the *Royal-Monceau* is a tempting alternative to the rather more stiff-necked establishments around the Place de la Concorde, the Alma or the Opera. For the category of its clients that may be called decision-makers – American, European, Japanese – it provides everything they expect of a good hotel, and adds to that the huge bonus of the peace and quiet of a private house. You sense this as soon as you enter the reception hall, one of the handsomest in Paris,

with its marble floors and tables, its Gobelins tapestries, its sedan-chair. The world may have changed, the clientele may have a different style from its predecessors, fax machines may be standard hotel equipment, but traditional values hold their own at 37 avenue Hoche.

Another suite. Catherine Deneuve was among the most enthusiastic supporters of this hotel.

THE TERMINUS SAINT-LAZARE

Atlantic gateway

The façade of the *Terminus Saint-Lazare* rises impressively between the arrival and departure forecourts of one of the largest railway stations in Paris. It is an immense hotel, a monument in the classical style, which can be seen to advantage by visitors returning from the great department stores on boulevard Haussmann just down the street.

Since the 1980s, two allegorical representations of travel, the work of the sculptor Arman, stand in the forecourts – in the cour de Rome "Consigne à vie", an design of suitcases cast in bronze ; in the cour du Havre a composition of timepieces, "L'Heure de tous".

The origin of this hotel is closely linked with that of the railways. It was built to accommodate travellers arriving at the station beside it (then in the process of reconstruction), with a particular eye to visitors coming for the *Exposition universelle*, held in 1889 to mark the centenary of the French Revolution.

The hotel and the station were both designed by the architect Juste Lisch. In placing the *Terminus* between the arrival and departure forecourts, he introduced the unprecedented concept of a luxury hotel in the immediate vicinity of a railway station. This arrangement was repeated eleven years later when the *Hôtel d'Orsay* was built into the station of that name.

For the convenience of travellers, Lisch linked the main hall of the station to the first floor of the hotel by a metal foot-bridge. This had many advantages, as is explained in a circular issued when the hotel opened : "People who travel a great deal must economize in three matters : time, money and energy. When you

step out of a train, you need a carriage to take you and your luggage across town, and another to take you back to the station when you are leaving. At gare Saint-Lazare, you walk straight into the *Grand Hôtel Terminus*, hand in your travel ticket and are already in bed while other less well-advised travellers are hanging around on the foot-path arguing with coachmen and porters.

When you are leaving, you do not have to lift a finger. Your ticket is brought to you in your room, you are informed when your train is in, and you cross the foot-bridge to your compartment without standing around in the cold, without fuss, and therefore without fatigue. You have been saved time, money and effort".

Under Juste Lisch's direction, the station and the hotel went up in record time, the hotel itself taking only fifteen months to build. All work was completed in 1889, and the *Terminus* opened its doors on the 7th of July of that year, within a few days of the unveiling of the Eiffel Tower and the launching of the *Exposition universelle*.

Today, you enter the hotel from rue Saint-Lazare, passing under a handsome awning into a great foyer decorated with mosaics and impressive pillars of pink granite. The immense hall taking up the whole centre of the building and now classified as a historic monument is one of the most spectacular in Paris, even though the stair-cases which used to lead to the foot-bridge are no longer there. It is surrounded by elegant cast-iron pillars carrying the ceiling and the glass roof. Between these pillars, on all four sides, there are two levels of galleries and balconies. At first floor level there is a frieze of cherubs pain-ted *en trompe-l'œil*, the work of the painter La-mire. All but one of the cherubs are facing for-ward ; to express his dislike of the hotel manager at the time, with whom he was on bad terms, La-mire depicted one of them seen from behind ! This splendid hall is crowned by a remarkable curved glass roof, and is further embellished by two enormous chandeliers which were among the first electric lights in Paris in 1889.

When the hotel opened, the publicity brochure boasted of the "marvels of refinement and mo-dernity" provided. Among these were numbered the three hydraulic lifts serving the five storeys, every storey having six bath-and-shower rooms. Other marvels thought worthy of special mention were "the telephone doubling the speed of ser-vice, the bell permitting the guest to be served without having to rise, the electricity which tells the time and provides lighting". Furthermore, according to the brochure : "Depending on its size, your bedroom will have either two or three electric lights. Should you be sitting at the fire, you have a light by the mantelpiece. Should you be at the table, you have a light overhead. When you get into bed, one switch suffices to put off the central light and turn on another beside you. You will think Houdini is at work".

Obviously, no hotel management anywhere in the world today would think of describing elec-tricity as something worked by magic, aome-

thing to be compared to a performance by the great master-magician himself. Yet it is a fact that hardly more than a century ago the *Termi-nus* was one of the first hotels to be lit entirely by electricity. All the furnishings for the hotel came from the *Grands Magasins du Louvre*, a sure guarantee of its quality. Ingenious lay-out gave the guest the feeling that everything was under his hand : telephone, cloakroom, separate lavatories for men and women, restaurants, even a shop where high quality travel goods were on sale.

The height of refinement was perhaps rea-ched by the provision of lockers which could be

Decorated ceiling, balustrades and granite pillars in the entrance hall are an excellent example of Classical ornamentation. A luggage label.

rented for the season. This amenity allowed the traveller arriving from the country to deposit his cloak and straw hat, and to change into his town coat and top hat.

At that time, the hotel had three restaurants – one of them serving *table d'hôte* meals only – as well as a wine bar. Guests were highly appreciative of the excellent food and fine wines. There was also a gourmet food shop, and a cellar of which the management was justly proud, with its venerable château Eyquems and its vintage burgundies.

The hotel records mention only one guest who was openly contemptuous of the fare served at the *Terminus*. In 1900 a pretty young Englishwo-

man remained in her room for several days, lying in elegant silk déshabillé on a chaise longue, and refusing all nourishment. The cause of her melancholia is not recorded, but we can be sure that it was not due to indigestion or food poisoning ! It appears that some of the staff talked of putting the lady on show as a strange spectacle.

During the nineteenth century, most of the clients at the *Grand Hôtel Terminus* were from the ranks of the idle rich or international travellers. There was of course the occasional dramatic incident during the period when anarchists were active in Paris.

On the 12th of February 1894, a bomb exploded at 8.52 p.m. at the *café-concert* in the

Terminus, killing one person and injuring twenty-two. Emile Henry, the anarchist responsible for the outrage, was arrested shortly afterwards in rue de Rome after having fired on his pursuers, wounding three of them. Henry, a young intellectual about to begin his studies at the Ecole Polytechnique, said that he had intended to kill as many people as possible to avenge the anarchist Vaillant, executed a few days earlier for having thrown a bomb at the Palais Bourbon. He added that he had chosen the *café Terminus* as a place frequented by "les bourgeois". A dramatic incident of a different kind was the flooding in 1910 when the Seine burst its banks and clients of the hotel had to be transported by boat.

The *Terminus* had many regular clients from the worlds of business and of letters. The famous playwright Georges Feydeau lived there from 1909 to 1919 and liked to sit in the main salon observing his fellow-guests. He was inspired by the atmosphere of his favourite

Detail of elaborate furniture typical of the hotel's style.
The French billiards room installed in 1930 has eight competition tables.
No other hotel in this category has kept a billiard-room.

The amazingly large
provision stores and
cellars were built early in
the century with an eye to
stylish organization.
Below : the brasserie at
the Terminus in 1992.

hotel to make it the setting for one of his plays, "Le Dindon".

In spite of the slump in the hotel business affecting luxury establishments in spa resorts, on the coast and in capital cities, the *Terminus* underwent a complete transformation at the end of the twenties. A fine billiards-room was installed in 1930 ; with its six tables it is still today one of the largest in Paris.

Between 1930 and 1934, the architect Henri Pacon put the *Terminus* in the front ranks of modern hotels. He designed a new *café Terminus* with a décor of white marble and globes in bronze frames. A jazz orchestra encouraged the latest dances. The new *Rôtisserie normande*, its design inspired by the transatlantic steamer *Normandie*, was an instant success. It was air-conditioned throughout and had indirect lighting in the central aisle. The columnist Curnonsky wrote that the beauty of the décor was equalled only by the quality of the food. The room is used today for conferences.

The Second World War put an end to this period of euphoria. In 1944, after the Liberation, the hotel was requisitioned by the Americans who called it *Grand Central Club* and used it to house Allied soldiers and hundreds of refugees. In the spring of 1946 the *Grand Hôtel Terminus* opened its doors once more to its usual clientele.

The staff has always lived up to its reputation for hospitality, and is remarkable for

the number of long-serving members. This was most evident at a reception given on the 22nd of June 1949 to mark the sixtieth anniversary of the *Terminus*. On that occasion the Minister for Labour publicly congratulated nineteen members of staff who had more than thirty years service, ten who had more than forty, and above all M.d'Hostingue, the chief accountant, whose name was on the staff list since the opening day, the 7th of May 1889 !

The hotel used to have 500 bedrooms. It now has just over 300, all of them more modern, more spacious, more luxurious. The management has high hopes that the hotel may enter the four-star category in 1993.

A great glass roof and gleaming chandeliers contribute to the charm of the great main hall. Note in one corner the splendid white marble fireplace.

THE TRIANON PALACE

Almost beyond belief

The *Trianon Palace Hotel*, as it has been called from the beginning, was officially opened on the 1st of May 1910. Among those present at the ceremony were Marcel Proust and Sarah Bernhardt, both of them to become regular visitors.

In the mid-eighteenth century, many estates were established by aristocratic families around the part of Versailles near the Neptune fountain and the grassland stretching as far as the Trianons. The three hectare park around the hotel had been part of such an estate.

Round about 1802, the horticulturist Charles Romain Féburier bought this park and planted trees which are still there today. In 1840, it was given to the bishop of Versailles, who used it to found a Capuchin monastery. During the first decade of the twentieth century, a development company acquired the property, cleared the site and employed the architect René Sergent to design a luxury hotel. Sergent put what can only be described as a château at the end of boulevard de la Reine, near the Trianons gate leading into the great park of Versailles and close to the fields where merino sheep have grazed since the days of Marie-Antoinette.

The new hotel was a bold architectural experiment. The body of the building is constructed on a metal framework, with masonry façades so carefully finished that they appear to be built of stone. In spite of what might seem disparate building materials, the effect is one of perfect harmony, a harmony affirmed in the corniced cupolas, the *alto-relievo* work, the garlands in the circular entrance hall and the Louis Seize motifs on the front face. The *salon Clemenceau*, originally the dining-room, with a floor area of

three hundred square metres, is in the Classical manner, as are the domes, pillars and arches in the gallery.

The plan of the hotel is quite simple : a main central structure with two wings roofed in the French style, with triangular pediments. The architect aimed at reproducing, especially in the interior, the décor and atmosphere of an eighteenth century house built in cut stone, in a happy alliance of worked stone, wrought iron and black and white floor tiles.

From its opening up to the present day the hotel has had a rich and colourful history. Fashionable society was not slow to discover this splendid hotel so near to Paris. In 1911, Gabriele d'Annunzio chose it as the venue for a dinner to which he invited three hundred guests. The carriages of the smartest Parisians were regularly drawn up outside.

During the Great War, the *Trianon Palace Hotel* was turned into an auxiliary hospital for British troops. In 1917 the Interallied Military Commission chose it as its permanent headquarters. Clemenceau, Wilson, Lloyd George, Foch, Pétain, Haig and Pershing often met there.

On the 7th of May 1919, Georges Clemenceau presented the Allies' peace conditions to the German plenipotentiaries at the hotel. The treaty determining the future of Hungary was signed there on the 4th of June in the following year.

After the war the *Trianon Palace* quickly recovered its fashionable status. A shuttle service by omnibus ran three times daily from its doors to the Place de la Concorde.

The twenties were the hey-day of luxury hotels, and the *Trianon Palace* reached new heights. There were days when there were so many cars and carriages outside that the porters had to use loud-hailers to summon chauffeurs and coachmen from the surrounding parkland.

Sarah Bernhardt used to come to lunch there. As soon as her carriage was sighted, the head porter would come out carrying a large screen to protect the great actress from curious onlookers. In the gallery, she would encounter Marcel Proust, always accompanied by his faithful Céleste Albaret, whose mission in life was to care for her master's health.

At the same period, André Citroën lived with his family in a first floor apartment looking out on the park of the palais de Versailles. While he was working on the development of the front-wheel drive, he used to go daily to his factory in quai de Javel in an ordinary production-line car. In the

Preceding pages : left, the great gallery at the Trianon Palace. Medallion shows letter-box in the foyer, in use since 1910.

Above, left : main courtyard and garden in 1910. At that time the hotel seemed remote from Paris. Even today, its woodland setting is a rest from the city.

mid-twenties, Cochet, Lacoste, Borotra and Brugnon, known as the Four Musketeers of French tennis, could be seen on the hotel's courts practising for the Davis Cup.

Gaby Morlay was a regular guest from 1922 to 1940. She enjoyed chatting with the staff. The wealthy Barbara Hutton always chose the same apartment on the first floor, and would sleep only in silk sheets which were the special care of one of the chambermaids.

"One morning in September 1925", says Henri Travers, a former head porter at the hotel, "we had a telegram from Le Havre announcing the arrival of John Davidson Rockefeller. The oil-baron and his two sons arrived that evening in an American embassy limousine. I immediately sent out two of my staff to attend to the luggage. Rockefeller held up his hand, saying : "No, no. I have these two strong boys with me. They are well able to carry their father's luggage". And so, under the gaze of people astonished to see such a lesson in humility, the heirs of the richest man in the world took up the suit-cases."

J.D.Rockefeller provided substantial funding for renovations at the palais de Versailles when it was in urgent need of repair. He liked to look in at the work in progress whenever he was staying at the *Trianon Palace*. The town showed its gratitude by making him an honorary citizen. All millionaires do not behave alike. At the Trianon Palace, the Vanderbilts, for instance, were plea-

Sacha Guitry during the making of the film "Si Versailles m'était conté", set in the château de Versailles. Many films have been made at the Trianon Palace, including "The Adventures of Arsène Lupin".

sant and generous, while Paul Getty, the shipping magnate, banker, oil-baron and collector, was felt to be very close with his money. Coming with his sons to the reception desk, he would say in gloomy tones : "Two medium-priced rooms, please". As if to justify himself, he would add : "I'm not a great one for comfort ; I'm never so happy as sleeping rough".

The most flamboyant client may well have been François Coty, a figure symbolic of the mood of the twenties. In 1928, the rich perfume manufacturer dismayed the world of journalism by founding a daily newspaper, "L'Ami du peuple" selling at ten centimes. Coty occupied two suites at the *Trianon Palace* for a time, together with his secretarial staff, his doctor and

The members of the Interallied Military Commission, seen here in the great gallery. From April 1917, the Allied Council of War had its permanent headquarters at the Trianon Palace.

Opposite : preparing to sign the Treaty of Versailles in the Clemenceau salon in May 1919.

his minder Frankel, an ex-boxing champion. During the Second World War, the hotel underwent varying fortunes. In 1939 it was requisitioned by the French and British armies. The Royal Air Force had offices there.

In July 1940 the Luftwaffe took it over. Into the *salon Clemenceau* came Field-Marshal Hermann Goering and General von Stupnagel, commander of the occupation forces in France. In 1942 Hitler come to a meeting at his staff head-quarters in the hotel. Besides the most extreme security measures, every precaution was taken within the hotel to ensure the visit would go off smoothly. For the occasion, the *salon Clemenceau* was renamed *salon Royal*. Hitler's staff had thought of everything...except one small detail. They had overlooked the marble plaque commemorating the outcome of the treaty of Versailles. Needless to say, it was immediately covered up. In 1944, the Allied Forces took over the hotel as their general head-quarters. The salons became conference rooms for Generals Eisenhower, Patton, Montgomery and de Gaulle,

The Clemenceau salon after 1992 restorations. One of the hotel diningrooms and the ballroom.

In the 1930s, J.D.Rockefeller stayed at the Trianon Palace, where he is remembered for his courteous manners and his generous funding of restorations at the château de Versailles.

while all available bedrooms and bathrooms were turned into offices. Only one place was safe from all disturbance : Mrs Eisenhower was left in peace to help her chef prepare light meals in her apartment on the first floor.

Peace brought back such regular clients as had survived the war. Though the time was past when maharajahs lived in suites that might have been settings for the Arabian Nights, the Aga Khan did return to occupy two whole floors, he in one suite, his wife in another, their secretaries and staff taking up the remaining rooms. Deposed kings came back as private citizens. Ex-king Umberto met Louison Bobet. Queen Maria Amelia of Portugal wrote her memoirs at the hotel, where king Farouk of Egypt might be found doing his accounts between two nights at the casinos on the coast of Normandy.

Most clients now made shorter stays, and very few took an apartment on a yearly basis. One who did was Maurice Druon, who wrote a substantial number of his books, including "Les rois maudits" at the *Trianon Palace*. In "Rendez-vous aux enfers", Druon writes about famous people who came to the hotel.

"Who can say how many writers took refuge there, to work safe from the importunity of tax-man or publisher, or how many politicians found solace there between two parliamentary sessions ? Illustrious feet have trodden those bright, peaceful corridors. Faces already familiar from illustrations in encyclopedias could be seen meditating by the high windows looking out on the park."

Visitors included Pierre Fresnay, Henri Bernstein, Edouard Bourdet, Marcel Achard, Joseph Kessel, Jacques Brel, Tino Rossi, followed later by Georges Pompidou, Valéry Giscard d'Estaing, Jean-Jacques Servan-Schreiber ; they all came to rest and enjoy surroundings favourable to creative effort or to reflection.

In its woodland setting, surrounded by the great park famous for its magnificent umbrella pines, the hotel was also a refuge far from prying eyes for those who were concerned above all with what Francis Carco delightfully calls "the cult of themselves" ; such people as the Duke and Duchess of Windsor, Jean Gabin and Marlene Dietrich, Sacha Guitry and Yvonne Printemps.

The hotel has pleasant memories of Sacha Guitry for his courteous manners and his liking for getting things exactly right. For his film "Si Versailles m'était conté", he even insisted on real

food – roast meats and elaborate set dishes – served in the most elegant of plates.

Mention must be made too of king Ibn Saud of Arabia, of the king of Morocco, of Queen Elizabeth II, of Habib Bourguiba, president of Algeria, and of Richard Nixon and Gerald Ford, presidents of the United States of America.

In 1967, the *Trianon Palace* was the scene of the press conferences of the Finance ministers of the great industrialized countries. Holders of a Nobel Prize regularly chose it for their meetings in the years following.

In February 1967 Richard Nixon was a guest at the Grand Trianon during an official visit to France. On that occasion the *Trianon Palace* played host to the largest contingent of journa-

lists it had ever seen. There were representatives from 700 international news media. Even the *salon Clemenceau* was barely large enough to accommodate them all for the press conference.

Between 1967 and 1970 the *Trianon Palace* offered something new to its clients and to the general public by running a series of concerts and candle-lit musical evenings with such performers as Georges Czifra, Roger Bourdin and Françoise Parot.

Several films were made there. Granier-Deferre, Suzanne Flon, Claude Brasseur, Brigitte Bardot, Maurice Ronet, Alain Delon, Marthe Keller and Georges Descrière all came to the hotel for "Aventures d'Arsène Lupin". In the film, the *salon Clemenceau* became a ball-room, another

Sarah Bernhardt was one of the earliest clients of the Trianon Palace, where Marcel Proust also used to stay. Below : an apartment redecorated during recent restorations.

of the lounges became an office in the Ministry of the Interior, and all the while vintage Bugattis were coming and going at the hotel entrance.

The *Trianon Palace* opened a new chapter in its history in 1990, when it was acquired by a large Japanese group. More than three hundred million francs have been expended on reconstruction and renovation work that took a year to complete. It is managed today by Albert Jean Ruault who began his career with Paul Bougeneaux at the *Plaza-Athenée*.

The hotel has been entirely transformed. It now has 62 bedrooms and 36 suites, three of them ultra-luxurious. All are equipped with state-of-the-art technology. In bedrooms and salons private fax-machines and computers can be laid on, video-conferences can be organized with participants all over the world, and 38 television channels with their teletexts can be viewed.

The renowned Versailles restaurant Les *Trois Marches*, run by Gérard Vié, is now accommodated under a wonderful glass roof opposite the gardens of the palace. There is a separate restaurant with the same chef, catering exclusively for special diets. The *salon Le Nôtre*, the *salon Clemenceau*, the *verrière Marie-Antoinette*, the *salon du Roi*, the *salon de la Reine* are all ideally suitable for conferences and colloquia.

The *Business Center*, dedicated to the memory of Paul Bougeneaux, is an integral part

of the *Trianon Palace*. Its function is to act as an international centre for economic and financial information. It is equipped with telex, computers, portable telephones, private and personalized fax machines, a multilingual secretarial service, and supplies apartments on request with facilities for video-conferences.

A sister hotel, the *Trianon*, has been built in the park, opposite the palais de Versailles, its architecture in keeping with the Classical context. The environment has been carefully protected and enhanced by specialist landscaping.

This new establishment has 197 bedrooms, all equipped with cable television as in the *Trianon Palace*. It has a multi-use hall seating 360 people, 5 committee rooms, a press room, public rooms, a *brasserie* which can seat 260 customers, a Japanese restaurant, and 4 "tatami" apartments opposite a zen garden and a piano-bar. The two hotels, the *Trianon*

The restaurant, a Mecca for lovers of good food, stands under its glass roof facing the parkland around the château de Versailles.

When President Nixon was General de Gaulle's guest at the Grand Trianon in 1969, seven hundred journalists attended the international press conference at the Trianon Palace.

The Spa, therapeutic baths centre under the gardens at the Trianon Palace since 1991, covers an area of 2,800 square metres and has a pool with a sun-roof.

Palace and the *Hôtel Trianon*, are linked by a landscaped walk.

One innovation at the *Trianon Palace* provides an amenity unique in the Paris region : the *Spa*, a hydrotherapy centre of 2,800 square metres. It is sunk below ground-level at the end of the terrace running outside the *salon Clemenceau*. Around the pool – focal point in the huge patio where clients can take the sun sheltered from the wind – there are gymnasia, therapy rooms, dance rooms, hairdressing salons, solaria, saunas, a restaurant for special diets and a traditional tiled *hammam* installed by a team of Turkish specialists.

Jean Courtière, president of *Parfums Givenchy* and of *Givenchy Couture*, has opened

a health and beauty centre, *l'Espace Givenchy*, in association with the *Trianon Palace*. Some of the services provided within its 1,000 square metres are open to the public, others are exclusively for residents in the hotels.

All these extensions, renovations and innovations have made it possible to receive a more diversified and more demanding clientele.

Which happily does not entail any diminution of the charm and tact that have been hall-marks of service at the *Trianon Palace* since the first day it opened.

The top floor bathrooms under the mansard roof are as luxurious as the rest.

197

SUMMARY

Acknowledgements

The publisher and the authors wish to thank the management and public relations services of the Great Hotels for their precious help during the production of this book.

Photographic credits

The following abbreviations indicate the position of each photograph in the page : t : top, b : botton, l : left, r : right, c : center

P. 6 : Coll. Bristol ; p. 7 : Coll. Pascal Boissel ; p. 8 (t) : Eric Brencklé/Demeures et Châteaux ; p. 8 (b) : Eric Brencklé/Demeures et Châteaux ; 8-9 : Coll. Pierre Jammet ; p. 9 : Gamma ; p. 10 (l, r), 11 : Eric Brencklé/Demeures et Châteaux ; p. 12 (t, b) : Coll. Pierre Jammet ; p. 13 (lb) : Eric Brencklé/Demeures et Châteaux ; p. 13 (lt, rt, rb) : Coll. Pierre Jammet ; p. 14 : Jacques Loyau ; p. 15 (t) : Coll. Pierre Jammet ; p. 15 (b) , 16, 16-17, 17 : Eric Brencklé/Demeures et Châteaux ; p. 18, 19, 20-21, 21 (b) : Affirmatif ; p. 21 (t) : Coll. Pascal Boissel ; p. 22, 22-23, 24-25 (t, b), 26, 26-27 (t,b), 27, 28, 28-29 (t, b) : Affirmatif ; p. 29 : Globe ; p. 30, 30-31, 31 : Affirmatif ; p. 32, 33 : Eric Brencklé ; p. 34-35 : Eric Brencklé ; p. 35 : Coll. George V ; p. 36 (t) : Keystone ; p. 36 (b) : Coll. Pascal Boissel ; p. 37 : Eric Brencklé ; p. 38, 38-39 ; Eric Brencklé ; p. 40 (b) : Keystone ; p. 40 (t) : Coll. George V ; p. 41 : Eric Brencklé ; p. 42 : Keystone ; p. 42-43 : Eric Brencklé ; p. 44, 45, 46-47, 48 (t, b), 49 (t) : Coll. Grand Hôtel ; p. 49 (b) : Coll. Pascal Boissel ; p. 50-51, 51 (t, c, b), 52-53, 54, 54-55, 55, 56, 56-57, 57 (tl, td) : Coll. Grand Hôtel ; p. 58, 59 : Eric Brencklé/Coll. L'Hôtel Hôtel ; p. 60 (t) : Douglas Kirkland/Sygma ; p. 60 (b), 61, 62 (t, b), 63 (t, b) : Eric Brencklé/Coll. L'Hôtel Hôtel ; p. 64 : Coll. Christophe L. ; p. 64-65 : Eric Brencklé/Coll. L'Hôtel Hôtel ; p. 65 (tl, tr) : Coll. L'Hôtel Hôtel ; p. 66, 67 : Françoise Masson ; p. 68 (tl) : J.-M. Marcel/Rapho ; p. 68 (tr) : Françoise Masson ; p. 68 (b) : Coll. Pascal Boissel ; p. 69 (t) : Coll. Intercontinental ; p. 69 (b), 70-71, 71 (t, b), 72, 72-73, 73 (b) : Françoise Masson ; p. 73 (t) : Harlingue-Viollet ; p. 74-75, 75 (t) : Françoise Masson ; p. 75 (b) : Coll. Pascal Boissel ; p. 76, 77, 78 (t, c, b), 78-79, 79, 80-81 : Coll. Lancaster ; p. 81 (t, c, b) : Coll. Bernard Etienne ; p. 82, 82-83, 83 (t, b) : Coll. Lancaster ; p. 84, 85 : Coll. La Trémoille ; p. 86 (t) : Robert Doisneau/Rapho ; p. 86 (b), 87 (t, b), 88 (t, b), 89 (t) : Coll. La Trémoille ; p. 89 (b) : Keystone ; p. 90, 90-91 : Coll. La Trémoille ; p. 92, 93, 94-95, 95 (b) : Affirmatif ; p. 95 (t) : Coll. Pascal Boissel ; p. 96 : Coll. Viollet ; p. 96-97, 98 (t) : Affirmatif ; p. 98 (b) : Coll. Viollet ; p. 99, 100, 101, 102 : Affirmatif ; p. 103 (t) : Coll. Sonia Rykiel ; p. 103 (c) : Harlingue-Viollet ; p. 103 (b) : Affirmatif ; p. 104-105 : Coll. Pascal Boissel ; p. 105 (t, b), 106, 106-107, 108 (tl, td), 109 (t, b), 110, 110-111, 111 : Affirmatif ; p. 112 : A. G. Emery/Coll. Pascal Boissel ; p. 113, 114-115 (t) : Coll. Meurice ; p. 114-115 (b), 115, 116-117 (t) : Coll. Pascal Boissel ; p. 116-117 (b) : Coll. Meurice ; p. 117, 118 (t) : Coll. Pascal Boissel ; p. 118 (b) : Marc Gaillard ; p. 119 : Coll. Bernard Etienne ; p. 120, 121 (t,b), 122-123 : Coll. Meurice ; p. 124 : Eric Brencklé ; p. 125 : Eric Brencklé ; p. 126 : Marc Gaillard ; p. 124-125 : Coll. Plaza ; p. 127 (t, b), 128 (tl) : Keystone ; p. 128 (b) : Marc Gaillard ; p. 128 (tr), 129 : Coll. Plaza ; p. 130-131 : Eric Brencklé ; p. 131 : Keystone ; p. 132 (t) : Coll. Pascal Boissel ; p. 132 (b), 133 (bl) : Eric Brencklé ; p. 133 (t) : Eric Brencklé ; p. 133 (br) : James Andanson/Sygma ; p. 134, 135 : Coll. Prince de Galles ; p. 136-137 : Coll. Pascal Boissel ; p. 137 (t) : Keystone ; p. 137 (b), 138 (t, b), 138-139 : Coll. Prince de Galles ; p. 140 (t) : Keystone ; p. 140 (b) : Coll. Pascal Boissel ; p. 141 : Coll. Prince de Galles ; p. 142 : Tauber/Coll. Raphaël ; p. 143, 144-145 : Coll. Raphaël ; p. 145 (t) : Coll. Pascal Boissel ; p. 145 (b), 146 (t) : Coll. Raphaël ; p. 146 (b) : Inge Moratt/Magnum Photos ; p. 147 (t, bl) : Coll. Raphaël ; p. 147 (br) : Black Star/Rapho ; p. 148-149 : Coll. Raphaël ; p. 150, 151 : Coll. Ritz ; p. 152 (t) : Coll. Viollet ; p. 152 (b), 153, 154-155 : Coll. Ritz ; p. 155 : Lipnitzki-Viollet ; p. 156 : Edimédia ; p. 157 (t) : Keystone ; p. 157 (b), 158-159, 160 (t, b) : Coll. Ritz ; p. 161 : P. Lorette/Catterine Feff ; p. 162, 162-163, 164-165 : Coll. Ritz ; p. 166, 167, 168 (t, b), 168-169, 170, 171 (t, b), 172 (t, b) : Coll. Raphaël ; p. 173 : Jacques Loyau ; p. 175 (t, bl, br), 176, 177 (t, b) : Coll. Royal Monceau ; p. 178 : Affirmatif ; p. 179 : Edimédia ; p. 180 (t) : Affirmatif ; p. 180 (b), 181 (t) : Coll. Pascal Boissel ; p. 181 (b) : Affirmatif ; p. 182 (l) : Coll. Pascal Boissel ; p. 182 (rt) : Coll. Terminus St Lazare ; p. 182 (rb), 183 (t, b) : Affirmatif ; p. 184 (t) : Coll. Pascal Boissel ; p. 184 (b), 185 (l, r) : Affirmatif ; p. 186, 187 : Coll. Trianon Palace ; p. 188 : Coll. Pascal Boissel ; p. 188-189 : Keystone ; p. 190 (t) : Cap-Viollet ; p. 190 (b) : Coll. Viollet ; p. 191 (t) : Coll. Trianon Palace ; p. 191 (b) : Roger-Viollet ; p. 192, 192-193 : Coll. Trianon Palace ; 194 (t) : Coll. René Dazy/Edimédia ; p. 194 (b), 195 (t) : Coll. Trianon Palace ; p. 195 (b) : Keystone ; p. 196-197, 197 (t, b) : Coll. Trianon Palace.